# Ironies and Complications of Free Speech

*News and Commentary From the Free Expression Policy Project, 2001-2017*

Marjorie Heins

D1495657

# Contents

# Introduction

The Free Expression Policy Project had its roots in the 1990s, when I served as director of the American Civil Liberties Union's Arts Censorship Project. In this job, I soon learned that the primary target of censorship in the United States is the subject of sex. There is something called "obscenity" that has long been assumed to lie outside the First Amendment's sweeping command that Congress shall make "no law ... abridging the freedom of speech." The big problem has always been how to define this "obscenity" exception to the First Amendment. Courts have tried various formulas over the years, without success: every definition has been impossibly vague and subjective. Justice Potter Stewart was honest enough to acknowledge this in 1969 when he simply wrote: "I know it when I see it."[1]

In other words, "obscenity" is a legal concept, yet it is impossible to define with precision. But that was only one of the ironies I confronted in my work at the ACLU Arts Censorship Project. There was also the more fundamental question: why is some subcategory of speech about sex (that is, "obscenity") unprotected by the First Amendment in the first place, while other categories that also occasion moral disapproval, such as racist hate speech and grotesquely violent entertainment, are fully protected?

This irony became particularly acute in the 1990s and 2000s, when media violence was at least as hot a target of censorship efforts as were explicit sexual images. Several states and localities passed laws restricting minors' access to violent video games. In the end, all of these anti-violence laws were struck down—as I chronicle in my commentary in this volume, "Why Nine Defeats Haven't Stopped States From Passing Video Game Censorship Laws." For the most part, the courts found that the laws were just too vague: they had the same problem of defining what it was the legislators thought dangerous as obscenity laws have always presented. That is, they didn't put people on fair notice of what was prohibited. Excessive vagueness has not proved fatal to obscenity laws, but, ironically, it has proved fatal to laws restricting media violence.[2]

I discovered something else in my days at the ACLU: a major social-political justification for censorship in Western culture has long been the notion that minors—initially, children, but by the early twentieth century also including teenagers—must be shielded from arousing images and bad ideas. I found this justification so intriguing, and so impervious to questioning in legislatures and courts, that I ultimately left the ACLU to write a book documenting its origins and development. That book became *Not in Front of the Children: Indecency, Censorship, and the Innocence of Youth*, published initially in 2001, and reprinted with a new introduction in 2007.

One thing led to another. Not only the touchy subject of "harm to minors" from exposure to literature, art, and entertainment, but myriad other issues of free expression policy—what is constitutionally protected; what is not; how to balance free speech against other values such as the separation of church and state—seemed to call for research, public discussion, and education, not just the continuing clash of opponents in high-profile legal battles. So I teamed up with my former ACLU colleague, Joan Bertin, who by 2000 was director of a small organization with a big mission: the National Coalition Against Censorship (NCAC). We created a think tank, as a part of NCAC, to provide empirical research and policy development on tough censorship issues.

We called our think tank the Free Expression Policy Project, or FEPP, and with backing over the next seven years from the Robert Sterling Clark Foundation, the Andy Warhol Foundation for the Visual Arts, the Rockefeller Foundation, the Nathan Cummings Foundation, and the Open Society Institute, FEPP published seven extensively researched policy reports, numerous friend of the court briefs in censorship cases, position papers addressed to administrative agencies, fact sheets, articles, news items, and reviews.[3] In 2004, FEPP moved from NCAC to the Democracy Program of the Brennan Center for Justice at NYU School of Law, where I worked on issues of structural media reform as well as continuing the traditional censorship beat. In 2007, a change in leadership at the Brennan Center led to FEPP's departure, whereupon I maintained the FEPP Web site as an informational resource up through the end of 2017.

## A Certain Concept of Free Speech

From the beginning, FEPP was not "absolutist" on the subject of free speech. For one thing, I never really understood what "absolutism" on this issue meant. There have always been legitimate and long-accepted exceptions to the constitutional "freedom of speech": libel and slander laws, invasion of privacy laws, laws prohibiting threats of physical harm, laws against blackmail and perjury. For another, the First Amendment is not the only part of the Constitution that articulates principles fundamental to democracy: to take just one example, subsequent amendments eliminating slavery and securing equal protection of the laws also create important rights that sometimes tilt the balance in favor of some restriction on speech. Balancing goes on, and necessarily must go on, in almost all matters of constitutional law and public policy.

As I wrote on the FEPP Web site:

FEPP takes a non-absolutist approach to free expression. For example, sexual and racial harassment, threats, and false advertising are types of speech that do not, and should not, have First Amendment protection. But a painting or photograph with sexual content is not sexual harassment; and a work of literature or scholarship is unlikely to constitute a threat. Speech may be offensive or controversial—but that is generally all the more reason to protect it. Unprotected speech should be narrowly and specifically defined, and have a direct, tangible, demonstrably harmful effect.

The point was to examine the fundamental values underlying the First Amendment, and ask how well our current public policies and legal rules serve those values. So, for example, if our goal is to have a fair, open political "marketplace of ideas" and an electoral system that is not marred by corruption, laws restricting massive spending on campaigns for public office are not necessarily unconstitutional. That is, more money may theoretically equal more speech, but countervailing values justify limits that prevent big spenders from drowning out everybody else. (The ACLU, my long-time employer, has long held the opposite view, although when I was an attorney there, many of us on the staff took issue with the ACLU's seemingly absolutist approach to this issue of campaign finance regulation.)

Similarly, in the increasingly fraught field of intellectual property or "IP" (copyright, trademark, and related laws), balancing is not only called for as a matter of policy; it is essentially mandated by Article I, section 8 of the Constitution (the Copyright Clause), as interpreted in light of the First Amendment freedom of speech. The Copyright Clause directs Congress to pass laws giving inventors, authors, and other creative folk monopolies over the copying of their works for "limited times," after which these works must enter the public domain and be available to all. And the First Amendment's "freedom of speech" demands exceptions to even limited-time IP monopolies in order to encourage so-called fair use: scholarship, commentary, parody, and other transformative borrowings of images and texts. By the mid-1990s, IP law and policy had blossomed into full-fledged censorship issues, as a result of a combination of huge congressional extensions of the "limited time" and aggressive claims of IP control by media corporations. Part Five of this book addresses some of the interesting, often troubling, and sometimes amusing issues that have arisen in the age of copyright control.

In January 2018, after several years of adding only sporadically to the FEPP Web site, I decided that it was time to bid it farewell. NCAC, now under the leadership of Chris Finan, was generous enough to post quite a few FEPP articles and court briefs, as well as all of its policy reports, on www.ncac.org, but much of the material was going to disappear from that all-important medium called cyberspace. I decided that some of the best pieces were worth preserving in book form, not only as a record of what transpired in the world of censorship and civil liberties in the years 2001-2017, but for information and policy arguments that are as relevant now as ever. They are relevant because the culture wars documented in the pages that follow are still very much with us, and the problems of defining free speech and its necessary limits (threats and harassment, for example) remain as thorny as ever.

I have organized this reader so that it can provide both an introduction to the ironies and complications of free speech, and intriguing case studies, for anyone interested in the subject, including, perhaps most importantly, high school and college students. The articles are arranged so that, along with this Introduction, they should provide sufficient political and legal background for those not yet initiated into the mysteries of censorship policy and law, and at the same time provide information, amusement, and food for thought for those readers who are already well grounded in the intricacies of the free speech universe.

## A Road Map

The book is divided into five parts. I start off with some basic questions about the meaning of "the freedom of speech," and how it's been applied in various settings, including academia and public employment. Part Two homes in on that inexhaustibly hot-button issue: harm to minors. The news and commentaries here encompass rock star Janet Jackson's infamous 2004 Super Bowl "wardrobe malfunction," the Federal Communications Commission's strangely anachronistic regime of censoring "indecency" on the airwaves, and the Supreme Court's dramatic new limits on students' free speech.

Confession: in college I was an English major. Today, I'm a volunteer tour guide at the Metropolitan Museum of Art. It was my love for art and literature that motivated me to initiate the ACLU's Arts Censorship Project in 1991. Part Three addresses some censorship incidents and issues in the realm of visual art, theater, music, and literature. A 2016 article, "The Notorious Women Artists of 1943," has its origin in my attempts at the Met museum to understand and talk to visitors about the momentous changes wrought by modernism in American art. As I delved into the research, I discovered that not only was modernism alternately celebrated and mocked by the public and critics at the time of its birth, but that sexism in the art world, and the consequent sidelining of female artists, was an intrinsic element in how modern art was promoted and admitted into the art history canon.

Part Four addresses private pressures for censorship, the media power wielded by large corporations, and the delicate balance between the free exercise of religion and the constitutionally mandated separation of church and state. Many long-time laborers in the free expression vineyards think that private industry control of information and entertainment, including the corporatization of our major universities, is the biggest censorship problem we face today. On the other hand, private, nongovernmental censorship, including self-censorship, can sometimes be a civic virtue, and in any event is often one element in the tangled web of considerations that we denote as editorial control (by newspaper publishers, for example), or artistic judgment (by gallery and museum curators). Even the ACLU has experienced private, internal censorship pressures, as my review of Wendy Kaminer's book, *Worst Instincts: Cowardice, Conformity, and the ACLU*, documents.

Part Five addresses the issue of intellectual property. I've outlined above why this is such an important component of free expression policy. (For further background, see also the essay "Structural Free Expression Issues: Copyright, Government Funding, and Media Democracy," in Part Four.) Creative practitioners of fair use continue to challenge or resist overreaching claims of copyright and trademark control, as illustrated, for example, by my reports on Google's attempt to ban the use of the verb "to google," and the failure by the owners of the copyright in Tennessee Williams's plays to stop transformative uses of perhaps his most immortal and tragic character, Blanche DuBois.

Not all copyright conflicts, however, end so happily for the practitioner of fair use. FEPP's policy report, *Will Fair Use Survive? Free Expression in the Age of Copyright Control* (available on the NCAC and Brennan Center Web sites), documents the many ways in which copyright holders intimidate fair users and chill free expression, including cease and desist letters and "take down" notices to Internet service providers.

Over the years, there were different contributors to the FEPP Web site, usually FEPP staff, occasionally outside guests. I was, however, always the major contributor, and I authored all of the articles in this volume. Going over them in 2018, I have found ways to update and improve them.

As this Introduction suggests, I found a good deal of excitement, amusement, and intellectual stimulation in my work for the Free Expression Policy Project, and I hope some of that experience will be shared by those who venture into these pages.

# Notes

1. *Jacobellis v. Ohio*, 378 U.S. 184, 197 (1969) (concurring opinion). The Supreme Court in *Miller v. California*, 413 U.S. 15, 24-25 (1973), announced a three-part definition of obscenity: "whether the average person, applying contemporary community standards, would find that the work, taken as a whole, appeals to the prurient interest"; whether the work "depicts or describes, in a patently offensive way, sexual conduct specifically defined by the applicable state law; and whether the work, taken as a whole, lacks serious literary, artistic, political, or scientific value."

2. Some courts also noted—as I discovered myself when I read up on the subject—that widely touted claims that scientific studies have shown fictional media violence to cause real-world harm were completely without substance. For more on this subject, see the Brief *Amici Curiae* of 33 Media Scholars in *Interactive Digital Software Association v. St. Louis County*, available at http://ncac.org/fepp-articles/friend-of-the-court-brief-by-33-media-scholars-in-st-louis-video-games-censorship-case, and the sources cited there.

3. The policy reports are all available on the NCAC Web site, www.ncac.org: *Media Literacy: An Alternative to Censorship* (2003); *Free Expression in Arts Funding* (2003); *"The Progress of Science and Useful Arts": Why Copyright Today Threatens Intellectual Freedom* (2003); *The Information Commons* (2004); *Will Fair Use Survive? Free Expression in the Age of Copyright Control* (2005); *Internet Filters: Revised and Updated* (2006); and *Intellectual Property and Free Speech in the Online World* (2007).

# Part One:

## What is "The Freedom of Speech"?

# Culture on Trial:
# Censorship Trials and Free Expression

For decades, "Banned in Boston" was a wonderful catch-phrase for improving book sales. But if Boston was a leader in literary censorship, the rest of America was not far behind. Especially when the subject was sex, government authorities competed for the distinction of banning works they thought immoral.

The bans were usually based on state or federal obscenity law. But what was "obscenity," and how were prosecutors, courts, and publishers to identify it? An English judge defined obscenity in 1868 as material that tends to "deprave and corrupt those whose minds are open to ... immoral influences" and that suggests to "the young of either sex ... thoughts of a most impure and libidinous character."[1] Courts in the U.S. followed this test for most of the next century.

"Obscenity" thus turned on the presumed vulnerability of youth. It wasn't until the 1930s that judges began to rebel against a legal standard that deprived adults of literature thought corrupting to children. The landmark case involved James Joyce's *Ulysses*.

## The Trials of *Ulysses*

In 1920, while *Ulysses* was still a work in progress, a literary magazine published its "Nausicaa" episode, in which the hero Leopold Bloom masturbates while watching a young woman display a bit of undergarment. The New York Society for the Suppression of Vice initiated a prosecution under the state's obscenity law. The trial judges were not impressed by expert testimony that described *Ulysses* as a brilliant work. One of

11

the judges refused to allow passages to be read aloud in court because there were females present (including the magazine's editors). "Nausicaa" was ruled obscene, and *Ulysses* was banned in the United States.[2]

In 1933, the publisher Random House challenged the ban by attempting to bring *Ulysses* into the country. U.S. Customs seized the book and filed a forfeiture application in federal court. The case was assigned to Judge John Woolsey, and the second trial of *Ulysses* began.

After studying the work, Woolsey ruled that despite its erotic passages and vulgar words, *Ulysses* did not violate federal obscenity law. Ignoring the traditional standard— whether the work would "deprave and corrupt" a vulnerable reader—Woolsey said the proper test of obscenity is whether the work would "lead to sexually impure and lustful thoughts" in a normal adult.[3]

The Court of Appeals for the Second Circuit affirmed, explicitly rejecting the vulnerable-child rule because it would suppress "much of the great works of literature." Although doubting that *Ulysses* was the masterpiece its admirers claimed, the court opined that "it is a sincere portrayal" of the "'stream of consciousness' of its characters," and was "executed with real art."[4]

*Ulysses* could now be sold in the United States, but it would be another 23 years before the Supreme Court followed the Second Circuit and rejected the vulnerable-child standard, announcing that the First Amendment does not permit government to reduce the adult population to reading "only what is fit for children." The Supreme Court then created a test for obscenity that turned on whether a work's dominant appeal was to the "prurient interest" of average adults, and whether it was "utterly without redeeming social importance."[5]

Although this definition of obscenity was vague and subjective, at least it recognized that adults shouldn't be treated the same as children. But the problem of children (and adolescents) remained. In 1968, the Supreme Court attempted to resolve it by inventing a "variable obscenity" rule under which "girlie magazines" and similar materials, even though protected by the First Amendment, lost that protection if distributed to minors.[6]

Then in 1973, the Court replaced the "utterly without redeeming social value" test with a new three-part obscenity standard for adults: whether the material was "patently offensive" according to "contemporary community standards," appealed to "prurient interests," and lacked "serious literary, artistic, political, or scientific value."[7] Although today this standard is generally thought to encompass only hardcore pornography, the vagueness and subjectivity of such terms as "patently offensive" and "serious value" leave a wide berth for prosecuting artists who may be the James Joyces of the future.

### Film Censorship and *The Miracle*

While courts in the mid-twentieth century were expanding constitutional protection for literature, movies were increasingly targets of censorship. States and localities established licensing boards empowered to ban any film they deemed "immoral," "sacrilegious," or otherwise "harmful." Using these free-floating standards, Chicago banned newsreels of policemen shooting at labor pickets; Ohio condemned a movie version of *Carmen* because women were shown smoking in public; Memphis refused to license a film that showed black and white children in school together.[8]

It was inevitable, though, that eventually the Supreme Court would acknowledge cinema's importance as a medium of expression. That point came in 1952, after New York State revoked a license it had issued for Roberto Rossellini's *The Miracle*, on grounds of sacrilege, after a pressure campaign from the Catholic Church.

*The Miracle* tells the story of a peasant woman who is plied with drink and then seduced by a vagabond whom she mistakes in her stupor for St. Joseph. When she becomes pregnant, her fellow villagers mock and torment her. Angry pickets from the Catholic Legion of Decency soon appeared outside the Manhattan theater where the film was showing. Francis Cardinal Spellman, head of the New York Archdiocese, called *The Miracle* "vile and harmful," insulting to "Christian faith and Italian womanhood," and communist-inspired.[9]

Accusations of communism were not unusual in 1950s America, when leftist screenwriters, producers, and workers of all kinds were blacklisted; and politicians attacked avant-garde art as communistic. But not all Catholics agreed with Cardinal Spellman. A group of Catholic intellectuals found *The Miracle* "deeply moving" and "profoundly religious." Rossellini himself protested that his intentions were pious: "'The Miracle' occurs when, with the birth of the child, the poor demented woman regains sanity in her maternal love."[10]

But Spellman was a powerful political figure; and the state Board of Regents, under pressure, soon revoked *The Miracle's* license. The film's distributor mounted a court challenge, not only to the vague and subjective "sacrilege" standard, but to the very existence of movie licensing. The state courts rejected his arguments, relying on a 1915 Supreme Court ruling that films were only a business, not protected by the First Amendment.[11]

It wasn't until 1952, with *The Miracle* case, that the Supreme Court finally recognized film as a form of free expression. The opinion in *Burstyn v. Wilson* first did away with the archaic ruling that cinema was not protected by the First Amendment; then ruled that "sacrilege" was not a permissible censorship standard. The word is too vague, the Court said, setting the censor "adrift upon a boundless sea amid a myriad of conflicting currents of religious views, with no charts but those provided by the most vocal and powerful orthodoxies."

But the Court left open the question whether states could impose prior censorship under a law designed "to prevent the showing of obscene films."[12] The decision in *The Miracle* case thus did not do away with film censorship. Licensing boards continued, using other vague standards like "immorality."

Then in 1965, the Supreme Court invalidated a movie licensing scheme because it did not provide for prompt judicial review.[13] Stripped of their freewheeling power to ban films without first going to court for a ruling on obscenity, the state and local censorship boards faded away.

The film industry also eliminated its self-censorship system in the 1960s. The Hollywood Production Code, which had operated in tandem with licensing boards ever since the 1930s, contained an extensive list of cinematic "dont's," including anything insulting to religion. During *The Miracle* case, in fact, the critic Bosley Crowther suggested that the Catholic Church made such a fuss over this limited-audience foreign art film precisely because foreign movies were not subject to the Production Code.[14]

## "A Pall of Orthodoxy Over the Classroom"

Accusations of communism were familiar by the time of *The Miracle* case, and teachers were often the targets. A 1949 New York law required the firing of any teacher belonging to an organization that advocated the forceful overthrow of the government. A group of taxpayers and teachers challenged the law, but in 1952 the Supreme Court upheld it.

That decision, in a case called *Adler v. Board of Education*, explained that tests of political loyalty for employment were justifiably designed to stop "subversive groups" from infiltrating public schools and poisoning "young minds." A dissent from Justice William O. Douglas protested that guilt by association was "a principle repugnant to our society," and that loyalty hearings would "raise havoc with academic freedom" by turning the school system "into a spying project."[15] Decisions like *Adler* did indeed give the green light to investigations of all kinds, where suspect teachers were asked about the books they read, the people they knew, and the nomination petitions they had signed.

It was not until 1967 that the Supreme Court reconsidered its endorsement of political tests for teachers. The new case was brought by Harry Keyishian, an English instructor at the University of Buffalo, and several of his colleagues. Each had refused to sign the state's non-communist oath. They challenged not only the oath, which had been created by the state university board of trustees, but mandates of the state's 1949 loyalty law, including the listing of "subversive" organizations, the disqualification of teachers who made "seditious utterances," and the rule that Communist Party membership was automatic grounds for dismissal.

The Supreme Court now struck down the 1949 law, explaining that vague words like "seditious" made it "a highly efficient in *terrorem* mechanism." It was not clear, for example, whether "the teacher who informs his class about the precepts of Marxism or the Declaration of Independence" would violate the law. In language that would be much quoted for decades afterwards, the Supreme Court proclaimed that the First Amendment "does not tolerate laws that cast a pall of orthodoxy over the classroom."[16]

*Keyishian v. Board of Regents* was a landmark decision, but it did not presage a smooth ride for academic freedom in the years ahead. Teachers' and students' ability to study freely inevitably conflicts with educational authorities' desire to inculcate their preferred values. In 1982, the issue again reached the Supreme Court, in a case involving the removal of books by Richard Wright, Kurt Vonnegut, and other prominent authors from a school library. The Court recognized school boards' power to remove books because of sexual content or vulgarity, but ruled that because a library is a "mighty resource in the marketplace of ideas," authorities cannot censor books for "narrowly partisan or political reasons."[17] This distinction between sexual content and political ideas sounded a familiar theme. Despite such precedents as *Ulysses*, the Supreme Court still could not see that sexual subjects might have educational importance.

The trials of *Ulysses*, *The Miracle*, and *Keyishian* were turning points in America's history of cultural censorship. Of the three targets—sex, sacrilege, and sedition—only the first remains today as an area where artistic expression can be officially banned. But efforts to censor religious and political ideas consistently reappear. From North Carolina Senator Jesse Helms's attacks on the artist Andres Serrano's photograph "Piss Christ" in 1989 to New York Mayor Rudolph Giuliani's attacks on the Brooklyn Museum a decade later because of artwork he considered "blasphemous," some government officials continue to try to silence art that offends their religious beliefs.

After the terrorist attacks of September 11, 2001, censorship increasingly took political form. Teachers and students alike were punished for statements that questioned U.S. foreign policy.[18] Wartime often leads to loyalty tests and impoverished political discourse. The courts have responded with occasional reminders of the First Amendment's importance, but often, long after the damage has been done.

Winter 2002

---

An earlier version of this article appeared in *Insights on Law & Society*, a publication of the American Bar Association Division for Public Education (winter 2002).

## Notes

1. *Regina v. Hicklin*, LR 3 Queen's Bench 360, 371-72 (1868).

2. See Marjorie Heins, *Not in Front of the Children: "Indecency," Censorship, and the Innocence of Youth* (2001, 2007), 40-41; Paul Vanderham, *James Joyce and Censorship: The Trials of Ulysses* (1998), 32-34; Margaret Anderson, *My Thirty Years' War* (1969), 174-75.

3. *United States v. One Book Called "Ulysses,"* 5 F. Supp. 182, 183-85 (S.D.N.Y. 1933).

4. *United States v. One Book Entitled Ulysses by James Joyce,* 72 F.2d 705, 706-07 (2d Cir. 1934).

5. *Roth v. United States,* 354 U.S. 476 (1957); *Butler v. Michigan,* 352 U.S. 380 (1957).

6. *Ginsberg v. New York,* 390 U.S. 629 (1968).

7. *Miller v. California,* 413 U.S. 15, 24-25 (1973).

8. As recounted in *Times Film Corp. v. Chicago,* 365 U.S. 43, 69-72 (1961) (dissent by Chief Justice Warren); see also Gregory Black, *Hollywood Censored: Morality Codes, Catholics, and the Movies* (1994).

9. "Spellman Urges 'Miracle' Boycott," *NY Times,* 1/8/1951, 1, 14; Alan Westin, *The Miracle Case: The Supreme Court and the Movies* (1961), 9; Bosley Crowther, "The Strange Case of 'The Miracle,'" *Atlantic Monthly,* Apr. 1951, 37.

10. William Clancy, "The Catholic as Philistine," *The Commonweal,* Vol. 53, 3/16/1951, 567; see also Otto Spaeth, "Fogged Screen," *Magazine of Art,* Feb. 1951, 44, quoted in *Burstyn v. Wilson,* 343 U.S. 495, 514-15 (1952) (Frankfurter, concurring); "'The Miracle' and Related Matters," *The Commonweal,* Vol. 53, 3/2/1951, 507; John Cooney, *The American Pope: The Life and Times of Francis Cardinal Spellman* (1984), 45; "Rossellini Appeals to Spellman on Film," *NY Times,* 1/13/1951, 10.

11. *Burstyn v. Wilson*, 278 A.D. 253, 258 (N.Y. S.Ct. 3d Dept.), affirmed, 303 N.Y. 242, 260-61 (1951). The 1915 decision was *Mutual Film Corp. v. Industrial Commission of Ohio*, 236 U.S 230 (1915).

12. *Burstyn v. Wilson*, 343 U.S. 495, 504-05 (1952).

13. *Freedman v. Maryland*, 380 U.S. 51 (1965).

14. Bosley Crowther, *supra*, 35. On the Hollywood Production Code, see Leonard Leff & Jerrold Simmons, *The Dame in the Kimono: Hollywood, Censorship, and the Production Code From the 1920s to the 1960s* (1990); Gregory Black, *Hollywood Censored: Morality Codes, Catholics, and the Movies* (1994).

15. *Adler v. Board of Education*, 342 U.S. 485, 493-94 (1952); *id.*, 509-11 (dissent by Justice Douglas).

16. *Keyishian v. Board of Regents*, 385 U.S. 589, 600-03 (1967).

17. *Board of Education, Island Trees School District v. Pico*, 457 U.S. 853, 870-71 (1982).

18. See National Coalition Against Censorship, "Free Expression After September 11: An Online Index," http://ncac.org/resource/free-expression-after-september-11th-an-online-index.

# The Redoubtable Karen Finley Confronts Georgia's Loyalty Oath

First Amendment advocates generally think of anti-subversive "test oaths" as archaic relics of an ignominious past, but the State of Georgia does not agree. When the performance artist Karen Finley, no stranger to bad laws, was confronted in 2008 with an old-style disclaimer of subversive affiliations as a condition of her accepting a job as a visiting professor at Georgia State University, she was appalled, refused to sign, and began to look for support within the faculty for a legal challenge to the oath.

Finley had been the lead plaintiff in a case decided by the Supreme Court ten years before—a challenge to a federal law requiring the National Endowment for the Arts to consider "general standards of decency" and "respect for the diverse beliefs and values of the American people" in awarding arts grants. Although the Supreme Court ultimately upheld this "decency and respect" law, it only did so by interpreting it to be essentially meaningless.[1] Nevertheless, the law served its purpose by intimidating the NEA into being very cautious with respect to future grant-making.

Finley, now a professor of art and public policy at New York University, had been invited to Georgia State as a result of her previous work in Atlanta: her participation in a group art show in 2007, her subsequent sold-out talk at the university, her performance of a work satirizing the first president, called "George and Martha," followed by an interview for the GSU journal *Five Points* and a lecture on America's involvement with Iraq, attended by more than four hundred students. Given this advance success, she seemed a desirable candidate for visiting professordom. But, sensitive to restrictions on free speech, freedom of conscience, and artistic creativity, Finley balked at an anti-subversive test oath of a type that she thought had been ruled unconstitutional long ago.

The oath is part of a "Security Questionnaire" distributed to all applicants for public employment in Georgia. Referencing the state's 1953 "Sedition and Subversive Activities Act," the questionnaire asks: "Are you now or have you been within the last ten years a member of any organization that to your knowledge at the time of membership advocates, or has as one of its objectives, the overthrow of the government of the United States or of the government of the State of Georgia by force or violence?"

If the applicant answers yes, she must name the organization and describe her "past and present membership status including any offices held." The form warns that a "yes" answer may lead to "further inquiry" and disqualification if it is determined that the person is a subversive within the meaning of the 1953 law.

## A Convoluted History

The Georgia oath has a checkered history. Test oaths of this type—in contrast to the more common and generally thought less objectionable "affirmative" oaths to support the constitutions of the U.S. and a particular state—became popular throughout the nation in the 1920s and '30s, when fear of communism became a convenient excuse for many politicians to attack liberal reformers of all sorts, including opponents of fascism, economic injustice, and race discrimination.

True, the Communist Party was active in the U.S. in the 1930s, often leading these reform campaigns and using them to attract new members and spread revolutionary doctrine. But there was no serious threat of communist revolution in the U.S., and the draconian punishments that many states imposed on public employees and others suspected of sympathy with communism, as well as the wide-ranging inquiries into their political associations, social lives, and reading choices, struck directly at the most basic democratic freedoms.[2]

Georgia was typical in this respect. In 1935, the state legislature passed a resolution requiring all public school teachers, including university professors, to swear not only to "uphold, support and defend" the constitution and laws of Georgia and the United States (a typical affirmative oath), but "to refrain from directly or indirectly subscribing to or teaching any theory of government or economics or of social relations which is inconsistent with the fundamental principles of patriotism and high ideals of Americanism."

In 1949, with Cold War hysteria mounting, the state added a more specific set of requirements: all public employees now had to swear that they were not members of the Communist Party, had "no sympathy for the doctrines of Communism," and would not lend their "aid, support, advice, counsel or influence to the Communist Party or to the teachings of Communism."[3]

It was not until the mid-1960s that a group of professors, represented by the Georgia Conference of the American Association of University Professors (the AAUP), filed a lawsuit challenging these two broad loyalty laws. The federal court in this case invalidated the 1935 requirement—for ideological conformity in teaching and personal belief—by pointing out the obvious: that the oath provided "no ascertainable standard of conduct," because "there is no definition of fundamental principles of patriotism or high ideals of Americanism and one would necessarily teach at his peril in the areas of government, economics or social relations." The oath was thus "unconstitutional and void under the First and Fourteenth Amendments to the Constitution."[4]

The anti-communist oath that was added to the law in 1949 fared little better in this case. Although the plaintiffs did not object to—and so the court did not rule on—the simple question about Communist Party membership, the court found the rest of the language to be unconstitutionally vague. It relied on two recent Supreme Court decisions striking down anti-subversive oaths in Florida and Washington; the Florida oath had language about "aid, support, and advice" to the Communist Party that was virtually identical to Georgia's.[5]

It took another twenty years for the disavowal of Communist Party membership to be eliminated. This resulted from an official Opinion of the state attorney general, rendered in response to a request from the secretary of state. The Attorney General's Opinion acknowledged that the federal court twenty years earlier, in the case brought by the Georgia chapter of the AAUP, had seemed to approve the simple requirement that employees disavow CP membership, but said that the court had not actually ruled on the issue. In the years since, the Supreme Court had struck down another state law, this time in Arizona, that deemed an employee guilty of perjury if she signed a standard affirmative oath of loyalty to the U.S. and the State of Arizona while "knowingly" being a member of the Communist Party or any other organization having for "one of its purposes" the overthrow of the state or federal government.

The Supreme Court said in the Arizona case that even "knowing" membership in the CP, a party that presumably aimed to lead a violent revolution at some undefined future moment if the time was ripe, is not, under the First Amendment, an acceptable reason to deprive a person of employment. That is, people may have joined the Communist Party out of sympathy with its position on civil rights, economic justice, the fight against fascism, or other worthy causes. As Justice William O. Douglas wrote for the Court in the Arizona case: "Those who join an organization but do not share its unlawful purposes and who do not participate in its unlawful activities surely pose no threat, either as citizens or as public employees." The Arizona law thus threatened "the cherished freedom of association protected by the First Amendment."[6]

Under this rule, people can't be deprived of employment or otherwise punished if they simply have knowledge of the unlawful aims of the Party; they must also have a "specific intent" to support those aims. This may have seemed like a fine distinction, but it basically meant that anti-subversive test oaths, to the extent they had ever been effective as a means of weeding out potential subversives, would now have to be phrased so narrowly that they would have little use apart from enforced rituals of political conformity. Most former and present members of the CP or other groups with revolutionary aims could now presumably disclaim any specific intent to support those aims without much fear of being prosecuted for perjury.

Given the Arizona decision and other similar precedents, the Georgia Attorney General ruled that Georgia's simple question about membership in the Communist Party is unconstitutional. Employment, the Opinion said, "may not be conditioned on an oath denying past, or refusing future, associational activities within constitutional protection. These protected activities include membership in organizations having illegal purposes unless one knows of the purposes and shares a specific intent to promote the illegal purposes."[7]

One might have thought that at this point, the Georgia legislature would have turned its attention to other matters, confident that its schools and other places of public employment did not need test oaths to secure their safety. But the legislators were undaunted, and instead now added the words "to your knowledge" to the language of their test oath. As the oath reads today—the one Karen Finley refused to sign—a potential employee must swear that she is not, and has not in the last ten years been, a member of an organization that "to your knowledge at the time of membership advocates, or has as one of its objectives, the overthrow of the government of the United States or of the government of the State of Georgia by force or violence."

Clearly, the legislature only partially fixed the problem. As the Opinion of the Attorney General explained, "knowing" membership is not enough to disqualify; the employee must also intentionally share in the unlawful aims of the organization.

If this all sounds convoluted, it is because in the early-to-mid 1960s, the Supreme Court chose to chip away incrementally at anti-subversive loyalty oaths, rather than attacking them head-on. But finally in 1967, the Court ruled more broadly, striking down New York State's elaborate system of loyalty disqualifications and investigations for teachers and professors. In this landmark case, Justice William Brennan wrote for the Court that the First Amendment simply does not tolerate laws that "cast a pall of orthodoxy over the classroom."[8] After this, it really seemed that anti-subversive oaths and statutes like Georgia's would soon become ancient history.

## Fear and Caution in Academe

But Karen Finley learned otherwise. And to her dismay, she found no eagerness among the faculty at Georgia State when she proposed bringing a legal challenge to the current law. In an effort to explore the issue and drum up support, Finley worked with Matthew Roudané, chair of the English Department and the professor who had initially invited her to teach at Georgia State, to organize a colloquium on loyalty oaths and their effects on artists. Among the speakers, in addition to Finley and Roudané, were Georgia State history professor Hugh Hudson, who presented a history of the state loyalty oath, and attorney Gerry Weber, who provided a legal analysis.

Yet there was no enthusiasm for a legal challenge. To the contrary: as Roudané told this author, everyone thought the oath was a joke, but no one was interested in joining a lawsuit. "Given the economy," he said, including furloughs—forced time off that effectively reduces the salaries of state university staff—"the last thing people want to do is get into a fight with the state."[9]

A year later, when Finley was finally considering going forward with the case on her own, with Weber as her attorney,

Roudané wrote that he could not provide a letter stating that the job offer to Finley was still open. It seemed that the Georgia State faculty simply did not want anyone raising the touchy, politically charged issue of loyalty oaths.

Ironically, the American professoriat was much more assertive on this issue sixty years ago, at the height of Cold War anti-communist furor. In 1949, about 300 professors at the University of California, most of them confirmed civil libertarians rather than communists, refused on principle to sign a test oath that singled out and stigmatized teachers as potentially disloyal. They eventually won their point in court, although the state legislature then simply expanded the oath to cover all public employees, and it was not struck down until 1967, in the wake of the Supreme Court decision invalidating loyalty programs in general.[10]

Similarly, Washington State's anti-subversive oaths, struck down in 1964, were challenged by a coalition of 64 professors. Even in the New York case that put the final nail in the coffin of broad state loyalty programs, five professors refused on principle to sign. (None were communists.) The lead plaintiff in that case, Harry Keyishian, later remarked that "there was widespread opposition" to New York's loyalty program among his fellow faculty at the University of Buffalo, but in the end, only five refused to sign the disclaimer oath. "Suppose there had been twenty-five, or for that matter five hundred? Clearly the problem would have been so serious that it is doubtful the administration could have taken any action at all. The faculty clearly underestimated its power and allowed itself to be stampeded into signing with unnecessary haste."[11]

Of course, the Washington and New York cases began in the early 1960s, a time when support for liberalism and respect for academic freedom were beginning to revive after the severe political repression of the 1950s. And the revolt of the California professors in 1949 can be seen as having taken place while liberalism was still fighting what turned out to be a losing battle against repression in the late '40s. One question raised by Karen Finley's unsuccessful effort to enlist Georgia professors in her challenge to the state's archaic test oath is whether we are now again in a period like the '50s, where silence, fear, and caution prevail in academia even though the outward signs of repression, such as legislative investigating committees and invasive loyalty investigations into people's associations, political activities, and reading choices, are absent.

A test oath, as Matthew Roudané pointed out, seems to many, perhaps most, people like a meaningless piece of paper rather than a problem of major civil liberties proportions. Certainly, there are few members of the Communist Party or other revolutionary groups in America today, so arguably, most people can sign such an oath without fear of being contradicted by informers and subsequently prosecuted for perjury. Only a few with conscientious scruples— Quakers and other religious objectors, for example—will refuse to sign, or so it is argued. Karen Finley is another, admittedly rare, example. But even if only a few are directly punished, the problem is significant: conscientious objectors are put to a cruel dilemma when they are forced to choose between their deeply held beliefs and a job to support their families— not to mention the loss to schools and students of good, sometimes great, teachers.

Karen Finley's planned courses at Georgia State, for example, were already fully subscribed when she was sent a packet of papers including the test oath. As a result of her principled refusal to sign, both students and faculty were deprived of exposure to her controversial, award-winning, intensely engaged feminist art.

But the problem goes deeper, and the chilling effect of test oaths of loyalty, although indirect, can be severe. The forced ritual of conformity puts everyone on notice to be careful about what they say, write, read, or in the case of teachers, teach. As the Supreme Court recognized in an early decision striking down a post-Civil War test oath, their fundamental flaw is that they violate the presumption that citizens in a democracy are innocent until proven guilty. Test oaths assume guilt and call upon individuals to establish their innocence; "and they declare that such innocence can be shown only in one way—by an inquisition, in the form of an expurgatory oath, into the consciences of the parties."[12]

A story recounted by Roger Revelle, a founder of the University of California at San Diego, illustrates the point. During the controversy over California's test oath for university professors, one of the oath's perhaps unlikely opponents, General "Howling Mad" [Holland M.] Smith, was asked by "a couple of the good ladies of La Jolla ... why those professors aren't willing to say they aren't communists. And General Smith said, 'Madam, if somebody asked you to take an oath that you were not a prostitute, what would you do?' They never spoke to me again."[13]

August 17, 2010

# Notes

1. *National Endowment for the Arts v. Finley*, 524 U.S 569 (1998) (holding that the "decency and respect" law is only advisory and has not caused any proven harm to artists).

2. See Marjorie Heins, "A Pall of Orthodoxy": The Painful Persistence of Loyalty Oaths, *Dissent* (summer 2009), for more detail on both anti-subversive test oaths and affirmative oaths of loyalty, and for the arguments pro and con.

3. See *Georgia Conference of the AAUP v. Board of Regents of the University System of Georgia*, 246 F. Supp. 553 (N.D. Ga. 1965).

4. *Id.*

5. *Cramp v. Board of Public Instruction*, 368 U.S. 278 (1961) (the Florida case); *Baggett v. Bullitt*, 377 U.S. 360 (1964) (the Washington case).

6. *Elfbrandt v. Russell*, 384 U.S. 11, 17, 18 (1966).

7. *Opinion of the Attorney General*, 1985 Op. Atty Gen. Ga. 48 (1985).

8. *Keyishian v. Board of Regents*, 385 U.S. 589, 603 (1967).

9. Nov. 13, 2009 telephone conversation with Matthew Roudané.

10. *Vogel v. County of Los Angeles*, 68 Cal. 2d 18 (1967).

11. Harry Keyishian, Unpublished paper (1965) (in the author's files).

12. *Cummings v. Missouri*, 71 U.S. 277, 328 (1866).

13. Roger R. Revelle, "Director of Scripps Institution of Oceanography, 1951-1964," an oral history conducted in 1984 by Sarah Sharp, Regional Oral History Office, The Bancroft Library, University of California, Berkeley, 1988, 7; see also Sylvia Tiersten, "Revelle," *@UCSD Magazine*, May 2010, 27.

# Of Threats, Intimidation, Sensitivity, and Free Speech: The Muhammad Cartoons

Countless words have been spilled over the Danish newspaper *JyullandsPosten's* publication last September of twelve cartoons commenting on journalistic self-censorship and Islamic beliefs, including several that caricatured the prophet Muhammad. Surely, everything has been said by now. Yet the controversy rages on: Is this an easy case for freedom of expression? Should there be no acquiescence in demands by some Muslim groups, backed up with lethal violence and threats, to suppress the cartoons? Or should sensitivity to intense religious feelings dictate self-censorship, or even government censorship, in the interests of saving lives and calming outrage?

Here are some basic facts and principles to help guide the discussion:

## Basic Principles: Violence and Free Expression

- Free speech, especially on matters of politics and religion, is essential to democracy. We can't have a free society if threats of violence (or actual violence) succeed in suppressing political or religious viewpoints, including satiric or "blasphemous" ones.

- Free speech is not "absolute": every society has restrictions. Some European democracies prohibit hate speech; the U.S. does not. We do have other exceptions to the First Amendment: for example, for "obscenity," "fighting words," and actual incitement to violence.

- What defines actual incitement? The words must be both calculated and likely to produce "imminent lawless action."[1] A good example is the familiar one of falsely shouting fire in a theater and causing a panic, because those in the audience are likely to react immediately, without time to reflect.[2]

- Insulting or offensive speech that triggers a violent reaction, by contrast, does not qualify as incitement. It isn't the speakers who are causing the danger; instead, it's the violent protesters. If violent reactions were a justification for censorship, then the most violent among us would be able to dictate what art, information, or ideas would be allowed.

## Defamation and Blasphemy

- "Group defamation"—false and insulting statements about a racial, ethnic, or religious group—was once punishable under U.S. law. But courts now recognize that this sort of exception to the First Amendment cuts too deeply into the free expression needed for democracy to work. The standards are vague and shifting: government censors would have a hard time agreeing on what ideas, images, or jokes about a religious or racial group are sufficiently insulting to be prohibited.

- Official restrictions on "blasphemy" or "sacrilege" infringe both free speech and freedom of religion. They inevitably discriminate against minority religious groups in favor of the dominant religion. As the Supreme Court explained years ago, they set the censor "adrift upon a boundless sea amid a myriad of conflicting currents of religious views, with no charts but those provided by the most vocal and powerful orthodoxies."[3]

## The Argument for Private (or Self-) Censorship

- A *New York Times* op-ed recently argued that although governments should not censor expression that's offensive to religious groups, the media should exercise editorial discretion and self-censor. In fact, the author said that this kind of self-censorship "is not just an American tradition, but a tradition that has helped make America one of the most harmonious multi-ethnic and multi-religious societies in the history of the world."[4]

- It is true that calls for self-censorship are frequent in the West; they are not unique to Muslims. Many groups in American society bring pressure to bear against TV and other media to avoid ethnic slurs, racist caricatures, homophobic stereotypes, and other insults—that is, to self-censor.

- Although this kind of self-censorship doesn't violate the U.S. Constitution—indeed, editors have a First Amendment right to decide what not to publish—the desire to avoid controversy for fear of offending any pressure group can lead editors to be overly cautious, can stifle creativity, and can end up silencing debate.

- For example, the Martin Scorsese film *The Last Temptation of Christ* offends some Christians and Shakespeare's *The Merchant of Venice* offends some Jews, but both are important works that contribute to our knowledge of history, including the history of religion and of religious intolerance.

- Editorial self-censorship is particularly problematic when it comes to questions of religion. Just as there are many variations on Jewish or Christian doctrine, so there are differences among Muslims on matters of belief. While some say that any image of Muhammad is sacrilegious, that image is found throughout Islamic and Arabic art.[5]

- Most U.S. media declined to publish any of the Muhammad cartoons, even though they have become a major international news story. Whatever the value of self-censorship, the public also needs to know what the debate is about. Widespread self-censorship by the U.S. mass media arguably encourages the violent protesters and isolates those few editors who have thought it their responsibility to publish the cartoons.

- Students in the U.S. have been filling the gap by printing articles pro- and con-, sponsoring forums on campus, and publishing one or more of the cartoons. At the University of Illinois, student editors were suspended for doing so. At Drexel University, they were deterred by threats of violence.[6]

## Should Highly Offensive Speech Be Silenced?

- Some have argued that the Muhammad cartoons are as offensive as anti-Semitic slurs, or Holocaust denial. Although offensiveness is always in the eye of the beholder, these comparisons are misleading. The cartoons were not aimed at ethnic stereotyping and did not deny historical facts. Instead, they sought to caricature political and religious beliefs.

- One reporter observed that initially, Danish Muslims found the cartoons offensive but bland. The two most controversial cartoons—one showing the prophet with a bomb in his turban and the other, the prophet calling out to suicide bombers, "Stop, we're running out of virgins"—

could be read as "comments on the manipulation of the faithful" by extremists. This writer suggested that it was really radical imams who were offended, and who circulated these cartoons and others throughout the Middle East in order to provoke demonstrations.[7]

• Even the most highly offensive speech, however, is probably better exposed and refuted, than driven underground. To paraphrase Justice Louis Brandeis: sunlight is the best disinfectant.[8]

February 22, 2006

## Notes

1. *Brandenburg v. Ohio*, 395 U.S. 444 (1969).

2. The example was given by Justice Oliver Wendell Holmes, Jr. in *Schenck v. United States*, 249 U.S. 47, 51 (1919).

3. *Burstyn v. Wilson*, 343 U.S. 495, 504-05 (1952). The case involved Roberto Rossellini's film, *The Miracle*, a retelling of the story of Christ's conception and birth which some leaders of the Catholic Church said was sacrilegious.

4. Robert Wright, "The Silent Treatment," *NY Times*, 2/17/2006, A23.

5. Andrew Maykuth, "Muhammad's Image is Far From a Rarity," *Philadelphia Inquirer*, 2/9/2006.

6. Monica Davey, "Student Paper Prints Muhammed Cartoons, and Reaction is Swift," *NY Times*, 2/17/2006, A14 (describing punishment of student editors at the University of Illinois). This article reports that student papers at the University of Wisconsin, Harvard, Northern

Illinois University, and Illinois State also published the cartoons. Editors at Drexel University published an editorial describing the threats that caused them to change their minds. "Editorial: Freedom of the Press?" *The Triangle Online*, 2/10/2006.

7. Jane Kramer, "Comment—Images," *The New Yorker*, 2/27/2006, 25-26.

8. Louis Brandeis, *Other People's Money: And How the Bankers Use It* (1913), 92.

# "What Ails the Agencies for Which They Work": The Parlous State of Public Employee Free Speech Law

The Supreme Court has taken a small step toward limiting the damage done to the First Amendment by its controversial 2006 decision in *Garcetti v. Ceballos.*

The Court in *Garcetti* denied First Amendment protection to a public employee (there, an assistant prosecutor) who had blown the whistle on police misconduct (in that case, fraudulent affidavits submitted to secure search warrants). The prosecutor was punished for writing a memo alerting his superiors to the fraud and then testifying to the same effect at a pretrial hearing. A majority of the Supreme Court ruled against the honest prosecutor because, so they said, "when public employees make statements pursuant to their official duties, the employees are not speaking as citizens for First Amendment purposes, and the Constitution does not insulate their communications from employer discipline."[1]

In last week's decision, in facts not very different from *Garcetti*, the Supreme Court ruled that because testifying in court was not one of the job duties of the director of a statewide program for underprivileged youth, the director had First Amendment protection against retaliation after he discovered, reported, and testified about illegal conduct by a state legislator who was on the payroll of the youth program. Instead, according to the unanimous Court in *Lane v. Franks*, the director's testimony was speech by a citizen on a matter of public concern, and therefore protected by the First Amendment.[2]

In reaching this welcome conclusion, though, the Court in *Lane v. Franks* ignored the facts that: 1) in *Garcetti*, the prosecutor was also punished, in part, for his testimony in court, and 2) in *Lane*, the director's report on the illegal conduct of the state legislator (for which, he alleged, he was subsequently fired) was well within his job responsibilities. Passing over these similarities, the Court's opinion in *Lane v. Franks*, written by Justice Sonia Sotomayor, emphasized that "information related to or learned through public employment" is often of great public concern: indeed, "there is considerable value ... in encouraging, rather than inhibiting, speech by public employees" because they "are often in the best position to know what ails the agencies for which they work."[3]

True enough, but Sotomayor also reiterated the Court's longstanding but dubious distinction between employee speech, as broadly described in *Garcetti*, and "citizen speech on a matter of public concern."

That distinction is a blurry one at best. As Sotomayor explained it, "the critical question ... is whether the speech at issue is itself ordinarily within the scope of an employee's duties, not whether it merely concerns those duties."[4] That's about as clear as mud; it's a form of words that seems almost infinitely malleable. Certainly, it is hard for public employees to predict when a critical comment or exposure of information that embarrasses the boss is "within the scope of" their duties or "merely concerns those duties."

Sotomayor's opinion for a unanimous Court in *Lane v. Franks* also had nothing to say about the scholarship and classroom teaching of public university professors, which is clearly "within the scope of" their duties but is also often of great public concern. This was an issue that surfaced in *Garcetti*, where Justice David Souter's dissent noted that the "ostensible domain beyond the pale of the First Amendment" that the majority described was "spacious enough to include even the teaching of a public university professor." Souter hoped that *Garcetti* did not mean "to imperil First Amendment protection of academic freedom in public colleges and universities, whose teachers necessarily speak and write "pursuant to . . . official duties."[5]

In response, the majority opinion by Justice Anthony Kennedy in *Garcetti* acknowledged: "There is some argument that expression related to academic scholarship or classroom instruction implicates additional constitutional interests that are not fully accounted for by this Court's customary employee-speech jurisprudence." Then, having acknowledged the issue, he proceeded to avoid it: "We need not, and for that reason do not, decide whether the analysis we conduct today would apply in the same manner to a case involving speech related to scholarship or teaching."[6]

Kennedy's ambiguous aside holds out some hopes that the Supreme Court's precedents recognizing academic freedom as "a special concern of the First Amendment"[7] will not be forgotten, but it does nothing to resolve the basic problem created by the Court's rigid but often unintelligible distinction between "employee" speech and "citizen" speech.

Judicial eagerness to keep petty disputes about job conditions out of the federal courts is understandable, but it has led to a pernicious doctrine of denying First Amendment protection for job-related speech by government employees that is often of great public concern (as was the case in *Garcetti*). The interest of the pubic in learning about the operation of government agencies should protect public employee speech against retaliation regardless of whether the speaker is thought to be acting as a "citizen" or an "employee." There is already a balancing test under the First Amendment for deciding when a public employer's interest in workplace efficiency outweighs an employee's interest in free speech and the public's interest in knowing "what ails the agencies" of government for which they work.

June 25, 2014

## Notes

1. *Garcetti v. Ceballos*, 547 U.S. 410, 427-28 (2006).

2. *Lane v. Franks*, 134 S.Ct. 2369 (2014).

3. *Id.*, 2377.

4. *Id.*, 2379.

5. 547 U.S. at 438 (Souter dissent).

6. *Id.*, 425 (Kennedy's majority opinion).

7. *Keyishian v. Board of Regents*, 385 U.S. 589, 603 (1967).

# Banning Speech in the Name of Fighting Terrorism

A majority of the Supreme Court yesterday rejected a First Amendment challenge to parts of a federal law that make it a crime to provide any organization designated by the Secretary of State as "terrorist" with aid in any of its activities, even lawful, humanitarian ones. The plaintiffs in the case included the Humanitarian Law Project, a human rights organization that wants to help the Kurdistan Workers' Party (the PKK) with training in peaceful conflict resolution through international law, and other nonprofit groups that want to assist the Liberation Tigers of Tamil Eelam, or Tamil Tigers, with humanitarian activities. But the PKK and the Tamil Tigers are both listed by the Secretary of State as terrorist groups.

The Antiterrorism and Effective Death Penalty Act of 1996, or "AEDPA," authorized the U.S. State Department to create a list of "foreign terrorist organizations"; then made it a crime to provide "material support" to any listed group. "Material support" was defined to include "training" and other forms of assistance, even if it was for peaceful purposes unrelated to terrorism. Terrorism was also defined broadly, to include virtually any actual or threatened use of a weapon against people or property. In making designations, the Secretary of State was directed to consider the "national defense, foreign relations, or economic interests of the United States."

The choice to label any group as terrorist is therefore a political and economic one. Violent regimes that torture and terrorize their citizens will probably not be designated if they are U.S. allies; and conversely, liberation fighters may be designated if they are trying to overthrow a regime that happens to be a U.S. ally, or where the U.S. has economic interests. For decades, for example, the African National Congress was listed by the Secretary of State as a foreign terrorist organization.

Congress amended the AEDPA several times, largely in response to court decisions striking down parts of the ban on "material support." The current version of the law specifies four types of "material support" that the plaintiffs in the case, *Holder v. Humanitarian Law Project*, argued are vague, overbroad, and otherwise in violation of the First Amendment. These four provisions, whose validity the Supreme Court has now upheld, make it a crime to provide:

- "training," defined as "instruction or teaching designed to impart a specific skill, as opposed to general knowledge";

- "expert advice or assistance," defined as "advice or assistance derived from scientific, technical or other specialized knowledge";

- "service," a term left undefined in the law, but according to the government's attorneys, any "act done for the benefit of " a designated group; and

- "personnel," which includes anybody who works under an organization's "direction or control," but excludes people acting "entirely independently."

In 2009, the U.S Court of Appeals for the Ninth Circuit found the first three of these four provisions to be unconstitutionally vague. The court explained, with respect to the ban on training, for example, that it "implicates, and potentially chills ... protected expressive activities and imposes criminal sanctions of up to fifteen years imprisonment without sufficiently defining the prohibited conduct for ordinary people to understand."[1]

But Supreme Court Chief Justice John Roberts's opinion yesterday said the terms are not too vague, nor do the material-support provisions violate the First Amendment: only a narrow range of speech is restricted, and even under the "strict scrutiny" required by the First Amendment, the restrictions are justified by compelling government interests.

Actually, Chief Justice Roberts's opinion did not subject the government's justifications to strict scrutiny; instead, it deferred to executive branch judgments about how to combat terrorism.

By contrast, the dissent of Justice Stephen Breyer, joined by Justices Ruth Bader Ginsburg and Sonia Sotomayor, did apply strict scrutiny. They agreed that the material support provisions are not unconstitutionally vague, but argued that the First Amendment does not permit the government to prosecute people for engaging in teaching and advocacy with lawful political aims, even if that teaching and advocacy is coordinated with a group branded as terrorist. This was because the government did not show that banning such peaceful advocacy is necessary to serve its compelling interest in fighting terrorism. All the activities the plaintiffs wanted to pursue involved "the communication and advocacy of political ideas and lawful means of achieving political ends," Breyer said. This "speech and association for political purposes is the kind of activity to which the First Amendment ordinarily offers its strongest protection."[2]

Breyer specifically took issue with Roberts's argument that even peaceful aid to a group like the PKK or the Tamil Tigers can further terrorism by lending the group legitimacy and allowing it to divert more resources to violence. Under this reasoning, Breyer pointed out, independent advocacy, uncoordinated with the terrorist group, could also be banned on the theory that it helps legitimize the group and buy negotiating time for unlawful ends.[3]

Because of the material-support ban, no U.S. lawyer could file a friend-of-the court brief for the PKK or the Tamil Tigers in this case, but several such briefs were submitted on behalf of other individuals or groups, including the Carter Center, established by former President Jimmy Carter to support international human rights, a group called Christian Peacemaker Teams, and thirty-two "Victims of the McCarthy Era," individuals or their family members or close friends who were blacklisted or otherwise lost their jobs, and in some cases served prison terms, during the late 1940s and 1950s, because of suspected associations with the Communist Party, even though they only supported the Party's peaceful aims, such as labor organizing and racial equality.

As a result of the blacklisting and other forms of political repression during the McCarthy period, the Supreme Court eventually ruled that people who had associated with a group deemed criminal or subversive could not be punished unless the government was able to show "specific intent"—that is, that they knew of and supported the group's unlawful aims. Much of the argument in the *Humanitarian Law Project* case turned on whether this precedent, which helped put an end to the anti-communist purges of the 1950s, should be applied now to the government's war on terrorism. Justice Breyer and his fellow dissenters argued that it should, but the Supreme Court majority was not persuaded. *The New York Times*, one among many critics of the Court's decision, editorialized that because the Supreme Court was not willing to apply the standard of specific intent in this case, Congress should now enact the standard into law.[4]

Law professor David Cole, who argued the case for the plaintiffs, said the Court's ruling would not only permit the government to prosecute anyone filing a court brief in support of a designated organization, but it might also allow a prosecution of former President Carter for such peacemaking efforts as meeting with Hamas and Hezbollah to encourage fair elections in Palestine and Lebanon.[5]

June 22, 2010

## Notes

1. *Humanitarian Law Project v. Mukasey*, 552 F. 3d 916, 929 (9th Cir. 2009).

2. *Holder v. Humanitarian Law Project*, 130 S.Ct. 2705, 2732 (2010) (Breyer dissent).

3. *Id.*, 2735-36.

4. "A Bruise on the First Amendment," *NY Times*, 6/21/2010, http://www.nytimes.com/2010/06/22/opinion/22tue1.html.

5. David Cole, "The Roberts Court vs. Free Speech," *New York Review of Books*, 8/19/2010, http://www.nybooks.com/articles/2010/08/19/roberts-court-vs-free-speech/.

# Is Teaching Junk Science Protected by Academic Freedom?

Ball State University in Indiana is embroiled in controversy over a course offered by its physics and astronomy department, called "The Boundaries of Science." The Freedom From Religion Foundation has complained that the course isn't science but religious indoctrination, and that because Ball State is a public university, offering the course violates the church-state separation required by the First Amendment.[1] Others say it's an exercise in academic freedom. In fact, it is probably neither.

Academic freedom protects professors' scholarship and teaching—within limits. It certainly protects the ability to broach controversial ideas in class. But it isn't an absolute right. Professors have to teach the subjects assigned, and can't engage in racial or sexual harassment, to mention just a few limits. There is also the matter of professional competence. A Holocaust denier may be competent to teach math or Spanish, but is unqualified to teach European history. A believer in "creation science" may be competent to teach medieval literature, but not biology. If the course is junk science, the professor has no academic-freedom right to teach it, and his department should have enough professional integrity to remove it from the catalog.

But what if the department decides not to? Does teaching the course at a public university violate the constitutional mandate prohibiting an "establishment of religion," as it almost indisputably would if offered at a public high school? There's little case law on this question—probably because there aren't many public universities that offer courses proselytizing religion under the guise of science.

The traditional formula for deciding whether a government program violates the Establishment Clause is the so-called "*Lemon* test," derived from the 1971 Supreme Court case of *Lemon v. Kurtzman.* The *Lemon* test asks three questions: whether the program has a secular purpose; whether its primary effect is to advance or inhibit religion; and whether it results in excessive government entanglement with religion.[2] More recently, the Supreme Court has used two other tests: whether the program amounts to government endorsement of religion, and whether it is coercive.[3] The coercion inquiry is particularly relevant to prayers and religion courses in public schools: where a prayer is mandatory, it forces students to recite beliefs they don't necessarily hold, and where a course is mandatory, it subjects them to possibly unwanted indoctrination.

In 1972, a federal court of appeals struck down a chapel-attendance mandate at a collegiate military academy, even though no one was required to attend the academy (unlike a public school) and even though cadets could be excused from the chapel requirement.[4] In two later cases, on the other hand, courts allowed graduation prayers at public universities on the theory that there was no coercion, there was a secular purpose (to "solemnize public occasions"), there was no primarily religious effect because "an audience of college-educated adults"—unlike school children—is not likely to be unduly influenced, and there was no excessive entanglement with religion.[5] But in a 2003 case, another court ruled that a supper prayer at the Virginia Military Institute did violate the Establishment Clause because the students were "plainly coerced into participating in a religious exercise."[6]

Then there was the strange case of a group in Nassau County, New York, which challenged a Human Sexuality course at the local community college because, they claimed, it "proselytizes against the Judeo-Christian sexual ethic and advocates an anti-religious sexual ethic to replace it." The judge found no endorsement of religion, a secular purpose, and nothing implicating any other part of the *Lemon* test.[7]

Clearly, the Establishment Clause cases are all over the map. How might these somewhat inconsistent precedents apply to "The Boundaries of Science"? There is no coercion because nobody has to attend Ball State or enroll in the course. There's little likelihood that reasonable observers would think the administration endorses the professor's religious message. On the contrary, a basic tenet of academic freedom is that professors don't necessarily speak for the university— indeed, they should be free to speak out against its policies. There's little chance of entanglement with religion, and although it might be difficult to discern a secular purpose, and the primary effect might be religious, on balance, the courts would probably not find this dubious course offering to violate the Establishment Clause.

Academic freedom, as a matter of First Amendment right at public universities, protects both the institution and the individual professor. The Supreme Court has noted the potential for conflict between the two. In the case of Ball State, though, the question is one of professional competence, and the institution, through its faculty committees, gets to decide whether "The Boundaries of Science" meets this standard. If it is religion masquerading as science, it clearly doesn't, regardless of whether it violates the Establishment Clause.

A case from the University of Alabama in 1991 supports this conclusion. Students complained that a professor of physiology was engaging in religious proselytizing in class.

The university told him to stop; the professor claimed a violation of his academic freedom. The federal court of appeals acknowledged that, as the Supreme Court had recognized years before, teachers' academic freedom is a "special concern of the First Amendment," but in the end ruled that the university was within its rights in restricting the professor's classroom speech. The court did not reach the question of whether religious proselytizing in a public university class violates the Establishment Clause.[8]

In the case of "The Boundaries of Science," the right of the Ball State administration to decide on the course's overall scientific validity is even stronger than was the University of Alabama's claim of authority to restrict a professor's occasional in-class proselytizing. The point is that these are educational decisions for the university to make, and absent a violation of the Establishment Clause, neither judges nor well-intentioned groups like the Freedom From Religion Foundation should second-guess them.

May 30, 2013

This article was also published in *Inside Higher Ed*, May 30, 2013.

## Notes

1. Scott Jaschik, "Science or Religion?," *Inside Higher Ed*, 5/17/2013, http://www.insidehighered.com/news/2013/05/17/ball-state-agrees-investigate-science-course-some-say-pushing-religion.

2. *Lemon v. Kurtzman*, 403 U.S. 602 (1971).

3.  *Lynch v. Donnelly*, 465 U.S. 668 (1984) (endorsement test); *Lee v. Weisman*, 505 U.S. 577 (1992) (coercion test).

4.  *Anderson v. Laird*, 466 F.2d 283 (D.C. Cir. 1972).

5.  *Tanford v. Brand*, 104 F.3d 982 (7th Cir. 1997); *Chaudhuri v. Tennessee*, 130 F.3d 232 (6th Cir. 1997).

6.  *Mellen v. Bunting*, 327 F.3d 355 (4th Cir. 2003).

7.  *Gheta v. Nassau County Community College*, 33 F. Supp.2d 179 (E.D.N.Y. 1999).

8.  *Bishop v. Aronov*, 926 F.2d 1066 (11th Cir. 1991).

# Charging Anti-Semitism to Squelch Dissent

Responding to complaints of anti-Semitism last October, the U.S. Department of Education began an investigation into anti-Israel protests at the University of California-Berkeley. The accusation was that the protests created a hostile environment for Jewish students. At about the same time, the California legislature passed a resolution defining anti-Semitism to include political rhetoric that characterizes Israel as a racist or apartheid state, or compares it to Nazi Germany.[1]

These charges of anti-Semitism carry unsettling echoes of American politics in the 1950s. In those Cold War days, calling someone a communist was so emotionally charged as to be unanswerable with logic. Essentially, there was no good response: for most of the American population, communism was as unthinkable and intolerable as anti-Semitism is today. The effect—if not the purpose—of the accusation was to demonize and silence political dissent.

Most Marxists, left wingers, and even members of the Communist Party USA in the 1950s were not unquestioning champions of Joseph Stalin or admirers of his tyrannical regime. People had moved left in the 1930s and '40s—and many had joined the Communist Party—because of their anger at injustice, racism, and poverty, their fear of fascism, and their frustration at the failures of American capitalism. Likewise, not all critics of Israel today are anti-Semites, and that includes those who use unfortunate rhetoric and offensive metaphors to condemn Israel's policies in the occupied territories.

It is easy enough to claim that political protest, which is often passionate and highly charged, creates a hostile environment for somebody, but the breathing space that free speech needs to survive can be readily suffocated by such charges, which fail to distinguish between the perceived offensiveness of the protesters' rhetoric and pervasive bigotry or discrimination.

It's true that equating Israeli policy toward Palestinians in the occupied territories with the Nazi genocide is a gross exaggeration and a particularly offensive form of political hyperbole, but it is not necessarily anti-Semitism—nor, as the California legislature would have it, is it necessarily anti-Semitic to "delegitimize Israel" or "apply double standards by requiring of Israel a behavior not expected or demanded of any other democratic nation."

Those examples—delegitimizing Israel or applying a double standard—come from a "Working Definition of Anti-Semitism" published in 2005 by the European Union Agency for Fundamental Rights.[2] The European group's definition has more caveats than the California legislature's, but is still too broad, because it conflates anti-Semitism— that is, bigotry against and irrational hatred of Jews as an ethnic group—with attitudes toward and characterizations of the State of Israel.

The evil of anti-Semitism remains a grave problem in Europe, where neo-Nazi groups continue to attract members despite laws banning their doctrines. Last March, a fanatic anti-Semite raided a Jewish school in Toulouse, France and killed three children and a teacher. The viciously anti-Semitic *Protocols of the Elders of Zion* circulates widely in Islamic societies.

But criticism of Israel—even advocacy of the unworkability of a Jewish state—is not the same as hatred of Jews as an ethnic group, just as criticism of capitalism, or indeed, belief in communism, was not the same as treason or conspiracy against the U.S. in the 1950s. During those panicky Cold War years, an argument commonly made against allowing communists to teach in public schools or colleges was that they were mental slaves of Stalin and had thereby abandoned all claim to intellectual independence. Even ex-communists were condemned unless they made lavish shows of repentance before legislative investigating committees or boards of education, which usually included "naming names" of others they had known in the movement for whatever time—whether years or just months—that they had been members of the Communist Party. Brilliant, dedicated teachers lost their jobs as a result of the purge; in many cases, their families suffered poverty, ostracism, and decades of police surveillance.

To be sure, a small minority of American communists in 1930s and '40s passed classified information to the Soviet Union or subordinated their intellectual freedom to Moscow. But the great majority did not, as evidenced by the steady rate at which people left the Communist Party when they found their disagreement with its frequently shifting doctrines sufficiently troubling to outweigh whatever combination of idealism and frustration had drawn them into the communist movement in the first place.

Today, it is widely acknowledged that the McCarthy era witch hunt against American communists, former communists, fellow travelers, and other leftists was a grave mistake—an abandonment not only of the academic freedom that's necessary for meaningful education, but of basic due process, free speech, and freedom of association. Reckless attacks against left wingers in the 1950s suppressed needed dissent over U.S. policies in ways that led our country into Vietnam and other post-Cold War quagmires, and that forged a Manichean pattern of thinking about foreign affairs that is still with us.

Charges of anti-Semitism leveled against critics of Israel are similarly repressive of political dissent. Regardless of one's view as to the two-state solution or any other aspect of the Middle East dilemma, more speech, not less, is needed if that tragic situation is to be resolved. As the president of the American Association of University Professors pointed out in a 2011 statement (responding to complaints from the Zionist Organization of America about anti-Israel protests at Rutgers University and elsewhere), the purpose of a university is to foster free speech—"to have students wrestle with ideas with which they may disagree, or even better, may make them uncomfortable. To censor ideas is to diminish education. ... By trying to censor anti-Israel remarks, it becomes more, not less, difficult to tackle both anti-Semitism and anti-Israel dogma."[3]

The effect of confusing vigorous, harsh criticism of Israel with anti-Semitism is, ironically, to nurture anti-Semitism. The more that unquestioning advocates for Israel fail to make the distinction, the more they encourage others to equate ethnic Jews the world over, whether or not religious and whether or not supporters of Israel, with the current policies of the Israeli state. And much as in the 1950s, at height of the anti-communist purge in academia and elsewhere in U.S. society, the effect of branding civil rights and other left-liberal causes as communistic was to undermine and discredit needed reforms, so today's accusations of anti-Semitism block clear-headed debate over the mess in the Middle East.

Especially at universities, which the Supreme Court once dubbed "peculiarly the marketplace of ideas,"[4] we should be skeptical when charges of discrimination or bigotry are aimed at political protest. The intense passions that anti-Semitism evokes and the gruesome history of the Holocaust make this a highly charged and difficult issue—but perhaps no more so than the demonization of American communists during McCarthy era. It would be a mistake to return to the path of smothering protest through irresponsible accusations.

December 23, 2012

**Update:** In 2013, the Department of Education closed its investigation of alleged anti-Semitism at three California campuses, finding that student demonstrations in support of Palestinian rights are First Amendment-protected speech that is especially important at a university, where "exposure to such robust and discordant expressions, even when personally offensive and hurtful, is a circumstance that a reasonable student in higher education may experience. In this context, the events that the complainants described do not constitute actionable harassment."[5]

But pressures to stop student protests continued, and in late 2014, a coalition of scholars and public interest organizations wrote an open letter to more than 140 universities warning them against bowing to pressures to limit campus political debate.[6]

# Notes

1. "U.S. Department of Education Probes Anti-Semitism Complaints at UC-Berkeley," *The Times of Israel*, 10/5/2012, https://www.timesofisrael.com/us-department-of-education-probes-anti-semitism-complaints-at-uc-berkeley/; Stephen Zunes, "California State Assembly Seeks to Stifle Debate on Israel," *HuffPost*, 8/30/2012, https://www.huffingtonpost.com/stephen-zunes/california-state-assembly_b_1842841.html; HR 35, Assembly Resolution, as amended, 8/23/2012, http://leginfo.ca.gov/pub/11-12/bill/asm/ab_0001-0050/hr_35_bill_20120823_amended_asm_v98.html.

2. European Union Agency for Fundamental Rights, (successor to European Monitoring Centre on Racism and Xenophobia), "Working Definition of Anti-Semitism" (March 2005), http://fra.europa.eu/en/publication/2011/workingdefinitionworkingdefinition-antisemitism (accessed 12/23/12). In December 2013, the European Union dropped its definition of anti-Semitism altogether. "EU drops its 'working definition' of anti-Semitism," *The Times of Israel*, 12/5/2013, https://www.timesofisrael.com/eu-drops-its-working-definition-of-anti-semitism. One commentator noted: "What damages credibility is seeking to equate criticism of bad behaviour by a powerful political entity to the daubing of swastikas and desecration of graves. Hats off to the FRA [the EU's Fundamental Rights Agency] for standing up for the fundamental rights known as free speech and freedom of the press." Mira Bar Hillel, "The EU has retired its 'working definition' of anti-Semitism—it's about time," *Independent*, 12/5/2013, http://www.independent.co.uk/voices/comment/the-eu-has-retired-its-working-definition-of-anti-semitism-its-about-time-8986565.html.

3.  "Anti-Semitism on Campus," Statement by AAUP President Cary Nelson and American Jewish Committee spokesman Kenneth Stern, April 2011, http://www.aaup.org/AAUP/about/officers/let/antisemitism.htm (accessed 11/28/12), as reported in Peter Schmidt, "Some Complaints of Campus Anti-Semitism Are Called Attempts at Censorship," *Chronicle of Higher Education*, 4/20/2011, http://chronicle.com/blogs/ticker/some-complaints-of-campus-antisemitism-are-called-attempts-at-censorship/32321 (accessed 12/23/12). The American Jewish Committee later disavowed the statement, and it is no longer available on the AAUP Web site.

4.  *Healy v. James*, 408 U.S. 169, 180 (1972).

5.  See National Lawyers Guild Press Release, "In Victory for Student Free Speech, Department of Education Dismisses Complaints," 8/29/2013, https://www.nlg.org/in-victory-for-student-free-speech-department-of-education-dismisses-complaints.

6.  CCR and Partners Inform Over 140 Universities That There is No Civility Exception to the First Amendment (Letter), 11/4/2014, https://ccrjustice.org/home/get-involved/tools-resources/inside-ccr/letter-ccr-and-partners-inform-over-140-universities. In September 2015, the Center for Constitutional Rights and Palestine Legal issued a report documenting hundreds of efforts to suppress speech critical of Israeli policies. *The Palestine Exception to Free Speech: A Movement Under Attack in the US*, Sept. 2015, https://ccrjustice.org/sites/default/files/attach/2015/09/Palestine%20Exception%20Report%20Final.pdf.

# In *Subversives*, It is the FBI, Not the Student Radicals, Who Subvert the Constitution

Review of *Subversives: The FBI's War on Student Radicals, and Reagan's Rise to Power*, by Seth Rosenfeld

Seth Rosenfeld, a San Francisco reporter, spent thirty years in Freedom of Information Act litigation against a stubbornly resistant FBI to obtain all the files that form the raw material for *Subversives*, his copiously detailed narrative of the Free Speech Movement at the University of California/ Berkeley in the 1960s, and of the FBI's many underhanded efforts to destroy it. Leading characters in this political drama are Ronald Reagan, governor of California from 1967-1975 and a longtime informer for the FBI; Clark Kerr, president of the sprawling University of California system—the quintessential man caught in the middle of the battle—; Mario Savio, icon of the student movement, gifted orator, and deeply troubled soul; and above all, J. Edgar Hoover, whose power as FBI director over more than 60 years enabled him to unleash his lengthy repertoire of dirty tricks against not only any group or individual he thought was communist-inspired, but also against liberal political dissent.

There are many intriguing, amusing, saddening, infuriating, and sobering moments in Rosenfeld's story— about Hoover's cozy alliance with Reagan, about his long, ultimately successful campaign to purge Kerr—a case study in slimy academic politics—; and about the struggles, strategies, and moral choices of Savio and a large cast of minor characters: idealistic activists, angry professors, conniving journalists, dubious informers, and fuming trustees. Rosenfeld's technique is to weave information from the FBI files into his account of the background and history of the Free Speech Movement and his portraits of its main protagonists—in particular, Reagan, Kerr, and Savio.

Occasionally, Rosenfeld makes facile biographical comparisons; for example: "Like Kerr on his Peace Caravans and Reagan on tour for General Electric, Savio was embarking on a demanding journey into new parts of the country to spread passionate views about freedom and democracy" (179). The reader hardly needs this far-fetched editorial attempt to link the life experiences of three such disparate characters.

But for the most part, the details are fascinating, especially Rosenfeld's rendition of Hoover's favors for Reagan over many years, from trailing his daughter Maureen, who had left home at eighteen and, Reagan and ex-wife Jane Wyman suspected, was living with a married man (148-49), to petty corrupt practices like selling Reagan a $19,377 armored Cadillac for a mere $3,000 (491), to a later incident during Rosenfeld's torturous Freedom of Information Act litigation, when the agency tried to redact the identity of another Reagan offspring, Michael, who was implicated in Mafia activities, from a document that it finally had to turn over. (Judge Marilyn Patel ruled that Michael's name was not exempt from disclosure under the FOIA exemption for "law enforcement activities," because it did not concern legitimate law enforcement but merely the FBI desire "to protect or promote Reagan's political career" [299].)

There are innumerable other tidbits that shed light on the actions and moral choices of characters in the ongoing political drama. The FBI files mention that Katharine Hepburn, a star not easily intimidated by the anti-communist purge in Hollywood in the 1940s and '50s, was "not a very high type" because she was living with the married Spencer Tracy (136). Hoover loved spreading sexual gossip like this—of course, anonymously: one 1965 memo recounts how agents exposed the "immorality" of an anti-Vietnam War activist by sending an anonymous letter to an anti-communist publication announcing that he had fathered "a son born out of wedlock" (311).

Other dirty tricks included plans to print a bumper sticker attacking movement activist Bettina Aptheker with the words "Bettina Craptalker for Governor," and attaching it to the bumpers of "appropriate communist-owned automobiles." Hoover's memo approved the idea but cautioned: "This must be handled in such a way as to completely protect the Bureau's interest. San Francisco should use all appropriate security measures in carrying out this operation so that this effort cannot be traced in any way to this Bureau" (313-14).

Talk about wasteful expenditures of taxpayers' money. This caper would be just an amusing footnote to history were it not so deeply representative of the lawlessness of the agency that did so much to cripple left and liberal protest throughout the twentieth century.

Rosenfeld's interviews with former FBI agents add further detail to the story. Burney Threadgill, Jr., was a particularly fruitful source. He told Rosenfeld that on one occasion he and a fellow agent were assigned to spy on a meeting at the home of radical journalist Jessica Mitford and her husband, the lawyer Robert Treuhaft; they hid in a crawl space underneath the house, and "as the meeting wore on, Threadgill fell asleep and began to snore loudly." The other agent quickly "rousted him and they crept away" (201).

Another agent, William Turner, who specialized in telephone taps, eventually became a critic of the agency; he later saw Mitford at a party, and knew he had heard that "mellifluous British voice" before. He approached her, explained that he recognized her voice and why, and said he even knew her favorite toothpaste (Ipana). "Mitford, characteristically, burst into laughter" (201).

Rosenfeld's narrative is scrupulously footnoted. In all of its 502 pages of text, I noticed only one error: he reports that James Meredith, with the help of a court order, finally succeeded in integrating Mississippi State University (342). In fact it was not Mississippi State but "Ole Miss"—the University of Mississippi.

*Subversives* is invaluable as history and makes for compelling reading. It adds detail to a story, however, that is already well-known, about the illegal conduct of the FBI over many years, culminating in its COINTELPRO program of spying and sabotage against the New Left. Nor does Rosenfeld grapple with the big questions raised by this history—among them, how deeply did it undermine democracy by stifling dissent and frustrating progressive change? To what extent is it responsible for the political stagnation we face today?

In January 2014, Margaret Talbot wrote in *The New Yorker*, apropos of Edward Snowden's revelations, that National Security Agency surveillance today, despite its breadth, is "nowhere near as disturbing as COINTELPRO's activities" were, because it is neither ideologically motivated (the NSA's actions were initially ramped up in response to a real attack; Hoover's were intent on destroying perceived enemies) nor thuggish (it entails surveillance but not infiltration or harassment or blackmail or smear campaigns). Yet in one regard—its technological prowess—it is worse.[1]

What Talbot does not mention is that, in addition to the vast technological scope of the NSA's data collection, police intelligence units today continue to spy on disfavored political and ethnic groups. Much of the detail of their anti-"subversive" activity is unknown. One hopes that it will not take fifty years and another crusade like Rosenfeld's to learn the full scope of government campaigns to sabotage political dissent today.

December 21, 2014

This review was also published in the journal *American Communist History*, Vol. 13, Issue 2-3, 2014.

## Notes

1. Margaret Talbot, "Comment: Opened Files," *The New Yorker*, 1/20/2014, 19-20.

# Part Two:
## Minors, Sex, and Violence

# Our Children's Hearts, Minds, and Libidos: What's at Stake in the COPA Case

Salon.com, Riotgrrl.com, and the "Kama Sutra" screen saver are just a few of the Web sites that are threatened with censorship if the Supreme Court rules against free speech in *Ashcroft v. ACLU*. This aptly named case—which the Court could decide any day now—challenges the 1998 Child Online Protection Act (or "COPA"), which makes it a crime to depict or describe sex or nudity on the World Wide Web if the words or images are considered "prurient" and "patently offensive" according to "contemporary community standards," and if they are thought to lack "serious literary, artistic, political, or scientific value" for minors.[1]

The last time the Supreme Court tackled this issue, it struck down the 1996 Communications Decency Act (the "CDA") because, by banning "indecency" online, it reduced the entire adult population of cyberspace to reading and viewing only what is considered "fit for children."[2] With COPA, Congress replaced the CDA's broad "indecency" test with a narrower "harmful to minors" legal standard. But the narrower standard still turns on the shifting conceptual sands of state or local community standards, "prurience," "serious value," and "patent offensiveness."

For example, what exactly is a "contemporary community?" New York City? Or Belzoni, Mississippi? State or local standards is a vague enough legal yardstick for traditional media, and an impossible one to administer in a medium that has an instantaneous worldwide reach. Because Web publishers can't restrict access to their sites based on geographic location, they run the risk of criminal prosecution unless they conform to the sexual tolerance level of the most puritanical city or town in America. When the Supreme Court heard oral argument in *Ashcroft v. ACLU* last November, the justices were acutely aware of this dilemma, and seemed inclined to resolve it by announcing that, at least for minors, America really has only one "contemporary community standard" for what is "harmful."

However the Supreme Court wriggles out of this legal mess, one thing it is unlikely to do is question the assumption that underlies COPA. The notion that minors are harmed by reading or viewing sexual material has had a firm hold on our psyches ever since the late sixteenth century when, as the historian Philippe Ariès writes, pedagogues began to censor bawdy classics and children were "taught to conceal their bodies from each other."[3] By the 1700s, pseudo-scientific tracts appeared in Europe detailing the pernicious effects of youthful masturbation—everything from pimples to madness and early death. It was a logical step to ban erotic literature on the grounds that, in the words of a famous English case, it might "deprave and corrupt" youngsters by arousing "libidinous thoughts."[4]

Today, the reasons for restricting youngsters' access to sexually explicit material tend to be much vaguer than fears of harm from masturbation. To most folks in our society, it just seems obvious that such material is inappropriate for younger children, and may give older ones the wrong ideas. But these are not the types of specific harms that are usually needed to justify censorship laws. In *Ashcroft*, the government's lawyers argue that no evidence of harm is necessary to uphold the law—it's enough that Congress wanted to foster the "moral development" of youth.

Laws like COPA certainly do send a message of moral disapproval to youngsters, but it's a hypocritical one, given the popularity of pornography among adults. Censorship laws do nothing to educate youth about sexual realities or sexual responsibility. In fact, they often perpetuate misinformation about critical issues like contraception, AIDS, STDs, and abortion, and silence speech about sexual orientation altogether.

Two journalists wrote in 1997: "There is no more enduring struggle in the culture wars than the one for our children's hearts, minds—and libidos."[5] If the Supreme Court strikes down COPA, Congress should stop passing Internet censorship laws and focus instead on education that can give youngsters the critical thinking skills they need to make sense of our sex-soaked culture.

April 18, 2002

**Update:** On May 13, 2002, the Supreme Court ruled that the use of an unpredictable "community standards" test to determine what online expression is "harmful to minors" is not in itself enough to invalidate the Child Online Protection Act. It sent the case back to the lower courts to determine whether COPA is unconstitutional on other grounds.

In March 2003, the U.S. Court of Appeals for the Third Circuit affirmed a preliminary injunction against COPA, ruling that the law's definitions of "harmful to minors" and "for commercial purposes" are too broad and vague to withstand the strict scrutiny required by the First Amendment for laws that restrict speech, and that there are less burdensome alternatives (such as Internet filters) that could shield minors from "harmful to minors" expression.

Again, the government appealed, and on June 29, 2004, the Supreme Court affirmed the preliminary injunction.

On March 22, 2007, after a full trial, Judge Lowell Reed of the federal district court in Philadelphia invalidated COPA on the grounds that it was vague and overbroad, and that voluntary use of Internet filters was a "less restrictive" way of shielding minors than a criminal law. On July 22, 2008, the Third Circuit affirmed Judge Reed's decision. On January 20, 2009, the Supreme Court sounded the death knell for COPA when it declined to review the Third Circuit's decision.[6]

An earlier version of this article was published on Alternet. org

## Notes

1. See *Ashcroft v. ACLU*, 535 U.S. 564 (2002).

2. *Reno v. ACLU*, 521 U.S. 844 (1997).

3. Philippe Ariès, *Centuries of Childhood* (1962), 113.

4. *Regina v. Hicklin*, LR 3 Queens Bench 360, 369 (1868).

5. Jeff Stryker & Maria Ekstrand, "Government to Teens: No Sex Education," *San Francisco Examiner*, 3/17/97, A17.

6. *ACLU v. Gonzales*, 479 F. Supp.2d 775 (E.D.Pa. 2007), affirmed as *ACLU v. Mukasey*, 534 F.3d 181 (3d Cir. 2008), cert. denied, 129 S.Ct. 1032 (2009).

# Supreme Court Carves Out a New Exception to Student Free Speech

In a fractured decision, the Supreme Court today approved the punishment of a high school student for unfurling a banner with the nonsense message "Bong Hits 4 Jesus" across the street from his school while the U.S. Olympic Torch Relay passed by.

Eighteen year-old Joseph Frederick insisted that his banner had no particular message except to assert his right to free speech. But Chief Justice John Roberts's opinion for four members of the Court in *Morse v. Frederick* said the banner could be "reasonably regarded as promoting illegal drug use," and that this was enough to override Frederick's interest in free speech. The Court also rejected Frederick's argument that his banner had full First Amendment protection because it was displayed off school property, and not at a school sponsored event.[1]

Roberts's opinion swept broadly, rejecting the traditional First Amendment standard for school censorship that the Court established in the famous Vietnam War era case of *Tinker v. Des Moines School District* thirty-eight years ago. Under *Tinker*, school officials can only punish student speech— in that case, black armbands opposing the war—if they have a reasonable basis to believe it will cause "substantial disruption."[2]

In 1986, the Court cut back on *Tinker* by allowing the punishment of a student who gave a sexual innuendo-laden speech at a school assembly. In Bethel *School District v. Fraser*, the Court said that the vulgarity of the speech justified censorship in the context of a school-sponsored event.[3]

In today's case, Chief Justice Roberts expanded on *Fraser* and essentially dispensed with the "substantial disruption" standard that a more liberal Supreme Court pioneered in the days of the Vietnam War. It was enough, for Roberts, that schools have an interest in deterring illegal drug use, and therefore banning any speech that might be interpreted to advocate it.

Justices Samuel Alito and Anthony Kennedy weighed in with an important concurring opinion that limited the breadth of Roberts's ruling in *Morse v. Frederick*. They joined the opinion of the Court, they said, only "on the understanding that (a) it goes no further than to hold that a public school may restrict speech that a reasonable observer would interpret as advocating illegal drug use and (b) it provides no support for any restriction of speech that can plausibly be interpreted as commenting on any political or social issue, including speech on issues such as the wisdom of the war on drugs or of legalizing marijuana for medicinal use."[4]

One can appreciate Alito and Kennedy's attempt to draw some lines here, and preserve some semblance of free speech for students, but their distinction between political commentary and advocacy of illegal conduct is not only historically flawed, it is completely tone-deaf to the way that teenagers, and indeed many adults, communicate their political views. Alito and Kennedy don't explain how, under their approach, school officials, students, or judges are supposed to distinguish between speech that "a reasonable observer would interpret as advocating illegal drug use," and speech "that can plausibly be interpreted as commenting on any political or social issue, including speech on issues such as the wisdom of the war on drugs."

Alito and Kennedy seemed to assume that everyone, including teenagers, makes neat distinctions between political discourse and silly slogans, or advocacy of illegal conduct. In the real world of social and political debate, slogans, banners, and what could easily be interpreted as advocacy of illegal conduct are inevitably mixed with more abstract or scholarly argument, including advocacy of changes in the law.

Alito and Kennedy were responding in part to a dissent by Justice John Paul Stevens, joined by Justices David Souter and Ruth Bader Ginsburg, that took Roberts to task for creating a new standard that "invites stark viewpoint discrimination" by allowing school administrators to suppress student opinions that depart from official policy. Stevens pointed out that "unfettered debate, even among high school students," is essential to democracy.[5]

One might say that it is *especially* essential among high school students, who are the verge of adulthood, and very much occupied with forming their identities and beliefs; who will soon be able to vote, and some of whom will soon be in the armed forces.

But Stevens, Souter, and Ginsburg undermined the force of their dissent by accepting that in public schools, officials may suppress student speech that "violates a permissible rule" or "expressly advocates conduct that is illegal and harmful to students." Their disagreement with the Court majority, instead, turned on their interpretation of "Bong Hits 4 Jesus." The banner, they said, "was never meant to persuade anyone to do anything."[6]

Thus, although Stevens, Souter, and Ginsburg started their dissent by condemning viewpoint discrimination in public schools, they ended by endorsing it—at least when the viewpoint expressed is interpreted to advocate "illegal and harmful" conduct. Like Alito and Kennedy, the dissenters don't try to grapple with the difficulty of distinguishing between political dissent and advocacy of illegal conduct, although they do point out that there have been many changes in public opinion and policy over the years: the legitimacy of particular wars, the prohibition of alcohol, and current debates over drug legalization are examples of areas where advocacy of illegal conduct has not been readily distinguishable from political dissent. Advocacy of sit-ins and freedom rides during the civil rights movement—both violations of then-existing state laws requiring or allowing racial segregation—readily come to mind as additional examples.

Justice Thomas, a rock-ribbed conservative on matters of minors' free speech rights (he doesn't think they have any) wrote a concurring opinion arguing that *Tinker v. Des Moines* should be explicitly overruled. Justice Stephen Breyer wrote separately to argue that the Court did not need to reach the ultimate constitutional issue because all it really had to decide was that Deborah Morse, the principal who punished Frederick for his banner, was entitled to "qualified immunity" from money damages.[7]

The fractured decision in *Morse v. Frederick* arguably represents another nail in the coffin of student free speech—which, like adult free speech, is often provocative or irresponsible—and another step toward a more controlled and authoritarian view of public education. However confused (and difficult to implement) the distinctions made by the Court, though, especially in the concurrence of Alito and Kennedy, there was at least a recognition that speech about drugs has a political dimension and that, in the memorable and much-quoted words of the 1969 *Tinker* decision, students do not lose all constitutional rights "at the schoolhouse gate."

June 25, 2007

## Notes

1. *Morse v. Frederick*, 551 U.S. 393, 127 S.Ct. 2618, 2625-29 (2007).

2. *Tinker v. Des Moines Independent School District*, 393 U.S. 503 (1969).

3. *Bethel School District No. 403 v. Fraser*, 478 U.S. 675 (1986).

4. *Morse v. Frederick*, 127 S.Ct. at 2636 (Alito and Kennedy, concurring).

5. *Id.*, 2649-50 (Stevens dissent).

6. *Id.*, 2644.

7. *Id.*, 2630-36, 2638-43 (Thomas concurrence).

# The Strange Case of Sarah Jones

Of all the odd "indecency" rulings that the Federal Communications Commission has issued over the years, the ongoing case of Sarah Jones and her rap poem "Your Revolution" is the most deeply suggestive of how censorship operates in America.

As many commentators have remarked, Jones's poem is explicitly feminist, deeply political, and a powerful critique of misogynist messages in both hip hop and rock music. (It's a remix of and response to Gil Scott-Heron's famous spoken-word piece, "The Revolution Will Not Be Televised.") For the FCC to brand this work as indecent and essentially ban it from the airwaves—as it did in May 2001 by imposing a $7,000 fine on the radio station that played it—betrays both the discriminatory nature of American censorship and the unwillingness of those in power to appreciate an artwork and a message that has particular relevance for young African American women.

Jones's rap poem, admittedly, has racy language. It starts: "Your revolution will not happen between these thighs," and continues:

> The real revolution ain't about booty size
> The Versaces you buys
> Or the Lexus you drives ...
> Your notorious revolution
> Will never allow you to lace no lyrical douche in my bush
> ... Your revolution will not be you smacking it up,
> flipping it or rubbing it down
> Nor will it take you downtown, or humping around ...

It's precisely the free (and imaginative) use of sexual language here that makes the rap empowering. As the DJ who played the poem at Portland, Oregon's public radio station KBOO, said: "Jones's song is inspirational. It says it's cool, you can be in the hip hop game, but you don't have to be no 'ho."[1]

So, where did an agency of the federal government get the power to censor racy language anyway? Expression that is nowhere near "obscene" within the legal meaning of the term, and therefore fully protected by the First Amendment?

The origin of the FCC's odd power to censor the airwaves goes back to the beginning of broadcasting, when it was necessary for some authority to assign different frequencies to different broadcasts so that their signals did not interfere with each other. Because of this initial need for licensing, and because the airwaves were thought to be a public trust, it was assumed that government has more power over broadcasting content than it has over newspapers or books. When the FCC started to assert this power in the 1930s, its targets were such terms as "damned" and "by God," as used by a radio orator. By the 1960s, the commission was still so prudish that it found wordplay such as "Bloomersville" (for Bloomville) to be punishable, and refused to renew the license of the offending radio station.[2]

There were no standards by which to measure "indecency," however, and by 1970, the need for a definition had become urgent. The FCC was continually threatening countercultural radio stations such as the Pacifica chain with indecency sanctions. To define indecency, it chose a case involving a Philadelphia station that broadcast an interview with Grateful Dead guitarist Jerry Garcia, who had complained on-air, among other things, that "political change is too fucking slow." The FCC, in punishing the station, now announced that indecency is any language it considers "patently offensive by contemporary community standards and wholly without redeeming social value."[3]

Five years later, in the famous "seven dirty words" case, the agency revised its standard and dropped the requirement that indecency has to lack redeeming social value. Now, ruling on a complaint about comedian George Carlin's famous "Filthy Words" monolog, which hilariously satirized taboos surrounding common four-letter words, the FCC said it would ban as indecent any language, no matter what its artistic value, that airs when a child might be listening, and that describes sexual or excretory activities or organs in a manner that's "patently offensive as measured by contemporary community standards for the broadcast medium." The offending radio station this time was Pacifica's New York affiliate, WBAI, which had broadcast the Carlin monolog as part of a program examining society's attitude toward language.

Pacifica sued to challenge the FCC's ruling, and won in the federal court of appeals, but in 1978, the Supreme Court reversed, and upheld the FCC's power to censor broadcasting under the indecency standard. The primary justification, wrote Justice John Paul Stevens for the Court's narrow 5-4 majority, was to protect kids, who the justices simply assumed would be "adversely affected" by George Carlin's bawdy language. Moreover, said the Court, the government wasn't really banning vulgar speech; it was only requiring that it be aired late at night, when children supposedly aren't listening.[4] Which is a bit like telling an artist to exhibit his work in a closet, or a writer that her book can only be sold after 10 pm.

Fast forward to 2001, when the FCC applied its broad, subjective indecency standard to another nonprofit, public radio station, for playing Jones's "Your Revolution." Language that's funny, inventive, and deeply resonant with inner-city girls and women was condemned as "patently offensive" and "designed to pander and shock." The FCC's cursory decision ignored the value of Jones's poem, and brushed aside station KBOO's explanation of the political meaning and cultural context of the work.[5]

With the help of People For the American Way, Jones sued the FCC for banning her poem from the airwaves. In September 2002, a federal judge in New York dismissed the suit for "lack of jurisdiction." The judge, Denise Cote, asserted that since the case was still before the FCC, it would be premature for a court to act. (The FCC is in the habit of issuing fines that can be appealed within the agency; then delaying any decision on that agency appeal indefinitely.)

Jones has appealed the district court ruling dismissing her case. She relies on a case decided seven years ago, in which jurisdiction was found to review the FCC's censorship regime. On the merits, though, two judges in that earlier case said the agency's practice of holding indecency findings over the heads of licensees for long periods of time was pretty bad, but not quite unconstitutional. One judge took issue with this lax approach to free speech, attacking the commission's "unbridled discretion" to police the airwaves, and noting that his colleagues' First Amendment analysis seemed "to border on the whimsical."[6]

Jones should win on appeal, but the courts tend to be reluctant to rein in the FCC. This has much more to do with politics than law. Censoring language under the broad, vague indecency standard would immediately be recognized as unconstitutional if the medium in question weren't broadcasting. But "patent offensiveness," standards of civility, and supposed harm to minors from vulgar words are still hot-button political issues. Even in this era where hundreds of cable channels compete for our attention with millions of Web sites (none of them hampered by indecency restrictions), the notion persists that broadcasting is uniquely subject to censorship because it is pervasive, "invades" the home, and may be easily seen or heard by children.

Thirty-three years ago, when there were liberal FCC commissioners, two of them dissented in the Jerry Garcia case, observing that "what this commission condemns today is not words but a culture, a lifestyle it fears because it does not understand." Jerry Garcia was not trying to titillate the audience, they said; "apparently this is the way he talks, and I guess a lot of others in his generation do so too."[7] Not much has changed, evidently, for their observations apply equally well to the strange case of Sarah Jones.[8]

January 24, 2003

**Update:** On February 20, 2003, faced with a possible loss on appeal, the FCC reversed itself and decided that "Your Revolution" is not indecent after all. Thus, it managed to avoid judicial review of its unbridled discretion to impose its conservative cultural standards on community radio.

## Notes

1. Deena Barnwell, quoted in Chisun Lee, "Counter Revolution," *Village Voice*, 6/20-26/2001.

2. See Marjorie Heins, *Not in Front of the Children: "Indecency,"* *Censorship, and the Innocence of Youth* (2007), 90-93.

3. *In re WUHY-FM, Eastern Education Radio*, 24 FCC 2d 408 (1970).

4. *Federal Communications Commission v. Pacifica Foundation*, 438 U.S. 726, 750 (1978).

5. *In the Matter of the KBOO Foundation*, File No. EB-00-IHD-0079 (May 14, 2001), http://www.fcc.gov/eb/Orders/2001/da011212.doc.

6. *Action for Children's Television v. Federal Communications Commission*, 59 F.3d 1249, 1263 (D.C. Cir. 1995) (concurring opinion of Judge Harry Edwards).

7. *In re WUHY-FM, Eastern Education Radio*, 24 FCC 2d 408, 418-23 (1970) (Nicholas Johnson and Kenneth Cox, dissenting).

8. Sarah Jones's Web site is at http://www.sarahjonesonline.com.

# What is the Fuss About Janet Jackson's Breast?

"If the flap over Jackson's stray breast serves to point up America's ridiculous censorship rules, this tempest in a B-Cup may turn out to be worth all the uproar."

                - Peter Howell, *Toronto Star*, 2/6/2004

The barrage of complaints about CBS-TV's broadcast of the Super Bowl on February 1 was, of course, about much more than the baring of Janet Jackson's right breast during the half-time concert. It was—at least so the pundits reported— about the coarsening of American popular culture: MTV suggestiveness, crotch-grabbing gestures by rock musicians, and uninhibited use of Anglo-Saxon words on the formerly "family-friendly" television airwaves. The fact that this coarsening was manifested during a sports event watched by hundreds of millions of Americans, adults and minors alike, probably accounts for much of the public outrage.

But attacks on the Federal Communications Commission's ostensibly lax enforcement of its rule against "indecency" on the airwaves were much in the news for weeks before the Super Bowl flare-up. In January, Representative John Dingell of Michigan, among others, pointedly asked NBC-TV why it did not bleep the rock star Bono's repeated use of a variation on the word "fuck" to express his exuberance during the live broadcast of the 2003 Golden Globes Awards (as in: "this is really, really fucking brilliant"). Representative Doug Ose of California introduced legislation to ban the "seven dirty words" from the airwaves no matter what the context. (The FCC bans them during all but late-night hours based on a vague and subjective judgment about context.) Senator John McCain has scheduled hearings for February 11 on "Protecting Children From Violent and Indecent Programming."[1]

It *is* curious, though, how mini-culture wars like this get started, particularly at a time when there are so many more pressing issues on the public policy agenda (the quagmire in Iraq, the Bush Administration's dissembling over weapons of mass destruction, the economy, even the question whether Howard Dean's primal scream was nonpresidential enough to sink his primary hopes). Indeed, one can't help wondering whether, confronted by all these serious issues, the brouhaha over Ms. Jackson's breast was simply a welcome bit of comic relief. Of course, ironically, mass media outlets stoke and reinforce the attacks against them by publicizing the cries of outrage.

The FCC's power to censor indecency on broadcast television and radio (that is, whatever it considers "patently offensive" as measured by "contemporary community standards") is a First Amendment anomaly. Speech that the agency considers indecent or patently offensive at any particular time is fully protected by the First Amendment, and may have serious political, artistic, or educational value. Yet the federal government claims power to suppress it, and the Supreme Court has so far agreed.[2]

The agency's record of enforcement has been as variable as the political winds. Until 1987, enforcement was lax, as long as broadcasters avoided the notorious "seven dirty words" that had been condemned back in 1978 in the Supreme Court case of *FCC v. Pacifica*. Pressures from the religious right in 1987 triggered a change: now, the FCC announced a "generic" test for patent offensiveness that would embrace sexual innuendo and double entendre along with taboo words. Of the three broadcasts the commission cited in this 1987 decision, two came from noncommercial radio: a KPFK-Pacifica reading from a play about homosexuality and AIDS, and a punk rock song played on a student radio station. (The third was a Howard Stern show.)[3]

Given the massive dominance of commercial over noncommercial broadcasting, the FCC's history of condemning nonprofit, alternative radio suggests that political appointees to a federal agency are the last ones who should be deciding what speech Americans will be allowed to hear. In recent years, the FCC has continued to apply its subjective "patent offensiveness" standard to suppress non-mainstream cultural expression such as the song "Your Revolution," by feminist rap artist Sarah Jones.[4]

If federal officials aren't the best choice for deciding what Americans can see or hear, then how do we address widespread objections to breast-baring, crotch-grabbing, and other Animal House behavior on television? The first response is that punishments by the FCC are not exactly going to put all of the vulgar words and lusty thoughts that cram our culture back into Pandora's box. Sexual explicitness in today's culture is a fact of life. Often, one can avoid it if one doesn't enjoy that sort of thing (though perhaps not on Super Bowl Sunday).

Parents cannot always block their children's eyes and ears, however; the best approach here has to be good media literacy education, sexuality education, and lots of independent alternatives to mass-market, lowest-common-denominator culture.[5]

On top of this, strengthening media ownership limits — rather than weakening them, as the FCC and Congress have been doing for the past two decades—could go far toward reducing the power of giant corporations like CBS/Viacom to decide what millions of Americans will get to hear, read, or watch (in this case, lots of raunchy entertainment and commercials, but *not* a political ad that criticized the Bush Administration, which CBS refused to air during the Super Bowl[6]). While the government should not be in the business of censoring media content, it does have an important role to play in structural regulation of the media industry. Breaking up the oligopolies can expand the diversity of ideas, viewpoints, and cultural styles that are available in the vast electronic and cyber world we now inhabit.

But the connection between media conglomeration and low-grade entertainment like the Super Bowl half-time event is not one that mainstream journalism is generally willing to make. When I suggested it to one reporter recently, he replied that since he worked for a media conglomerate himself, that part of our interview was unlikely to make it into his story.

February 3, 2004

An earlier version of this essay was published in *Quest: Reading the World and Arguing for Change* (2007).

**Update:** In 2006, broadcast companies filed a court challenge to a new FCC rule that, in most circumstances, bans even one "fleeting expletive" from the airwaves. In 2007, the U.S. Court of Appeals for the Second Circuit struck down this "fleeting expletives" rule as "arbitrary and capricious," but the Supreme Court reversed, and sent the case back to the Second Circuit to decide whether the rule violated the First

Amendment. In 2010, the Second Circuit struck down the FCC's entire indecency policy as unconstitutionally vague.

On June 27, 2011, however, the Supreme Court granted the government's petition for review of the Court of Appeals ruling, as well as another Second Circuit decision that struck down an indecency finding against the popular TV show *NYPD Blue*, for showing a few moments of female nudity. On June 21, 2012, the Supreme Court vacated the FCC's orders on narrow due process grounds, without reaching the First Amendment issues.[7] The long drawn-out litigation challenging the FCC's indecency regime thus ended not with a bang but a whimper.[8]

## Notes

1. See Marjorie Heins, *Not in Front of the Children: "Indecency," Censorship, and the Innocence of Youth* (2d ed., 2007), xvi-xx; Edward Epstein, "GOP representative would ban dirty words from TV," *SF Gate*, 1/9/2004, http://www.sfgate.com/news/article/GOP-representative-would-ban-dirty-words-from-TV-2815406.php; Senate Hearing, 108th Cong., 2d Sess., Committee on Commerce, Science, and Transportation, "Protecting Children From Violent and Indecent Programming," 2/11/2004.

2. The Supreme Court case upholding the FCC's power to censor "indecency" is *FCC v. Pacifica Foundation*, 438 U.S. 726 (1978).

3. See Heins, *Not in Front of the Children, supra*, 109-13, for discussion and citations.

4. See "The Strange Case of Sarah Jones" in this volume.

5. See *Media Literacy: An Alternative to Censorship* (Free Expression Policy Project, 2003), http://ncac.org/fepp-articles/media-literacy-an-alternative-to-censorship.

6. Jonathan Darman, "Censored at the Super Bowl," *Newsweek*, 1/30/2004, https://web.archive.org/web/20040309180112/ http://www.msnbc.msn.com/id/4114703.

7. *FCC v. Fox Television Stations*, 132 S.Ct. 2307 (2012).

8. See "Sarcasm Reigns as Court of Appeals Revisits the FCC's "Fleeting Expletives" Rule," in this volume.

# Sarcasm Reigns as Court of Appeals Revisits the FCC's "Fleeting Expletives" Rule

Three federal judges today subjected a lawyer for the Federal Communications Commission to a barrage of withering sarcasm during oral argument in round three of *Fox Television v. FCC*, the broadcast industry's constitutional challenge to the agency's rule that presumptively bans even one "fleeting expletive" from the airwaves.

Judge Rosemary Pooler, presiding at the argument before the U.S. Court of Appeals for the Second Circuit, repeatedly mocked FCC attorney Jacob Lewis's claim that the agency's policy of "bending over backwards" to respect the editorial discretion of producers is sufficient to avoid the obvious First Amendment problems with its broad, vague, and subjective regime of punishing broadcasters for programming that it considers "indecent." Judge Pierre Leval, joining in the action, characterized the FCC's censorship regime as a "vast miasma" that chills all manner of valuable programming because of the agency's shifting and unpredictable censorship decisions.

Peter Hall, the third judge, was less vocal but suggested, as he had in 2006 when the case was first argued, that it is essentially irrational for the FCC to punish fleeting expletives when uttered by celebrities during televised music award programs, but not when the same expletives are repeated in news reports.

This case has its origins in a 2004 ruling by the FCC that the rock star Bono's exclamation, "this is really fucking brilliant!" at a televised Golden Globes Award ceremony violated the agency's rule against indecency, even though previously it had said that a "fleeting expletive" on radio or broadcast television would not be punished. The next year, the FCC backed off when it gave a pass to director Steven Spielberg's patriotic film *Saving Private Ryan* despite pervasive expletives. Although even one expletive is presumptively indecent, the FCC commissioners said, in the case of *Saving Private Ryan* the rough language was necessary to the film's artistic purpose.

In a March 2006 "Omnibus Order," however, the FCC would not accord the same artistic deference to director Martin Scorsese's documentary on the blues, which had been broadcast on PBS stations. This time the commissioners thought the expletives used by some of those interviewed for the film weren't necessary to its artistic purpose and should have been left on the cutting room floor.

Such second-guessing of artistic judgments was another repeated theme of Judge Pooler's at today's oral argument. Agreeing with attorney Miguel Estrada, who argued for NBC-Universal, that the FCC's "indecency" policy is too vague and subjective to comply with the First Amendment, she said, "That's why *Saving Private Ryan* gets in and *The Blues* does not?"

Estrada replied: "Exactly." The First Amendment, he said, doesn't permit "unbridled discretion" by government officials. Here, "we have an undeniable record of arbitrary enforcement. We like Spielberg but don't much care for Scorsese. That's not an acceptable First Amendment standard."

The broadcast industry brought a legal challenge to four parts of the 2006 Omnibus Order: indecency findings against an episode of *NYPD Blue* in which Detective Sipowitz used the term "bullshit"—though the agency said his use "dickhead" was OK (I am not kidding); a segment of *The Early Show* in which a reality show contestant referred to a fellow contestant as a "bullshitter"; a Billboard Music Awards show in which the actress Cher said "fuck 'em" in referring to people who thought her career was over; and the same program the following year, in which entertainer Nicole Richie commented: "Have you ever tried to get cow shit out of a Prada purse? It's not so fucking simple."

After the networks' lawsuit was filed, the FCC persuaded the court to stay proceedings pending a reconsideration of the rulings against *NYPD Blue*, *The Early Show*, and the two Billboards award shows. The obvious purpose was to enable the agency to reverse itself on those rulings that seemed most vulnerable to a constitutional challenge. Sure enough, the FCC now conveniently changed its mind about *NYPD Blue* and *The Early Show*, thus leaving only the two Billboard programs with findings of indecency that the networks and others participating in the lawsuit could challenge.

Still, when the case got back to the Second Circuit Court of Appeals, it had before it a record of all the FCC's contradictions and about-faces, including the striking difference between its treatment of Spielberg's *Saving Private Ryan* and Scorsese's *The Blues*. What followed, in 2007, was a decision by the same three judges who heard oral argument today, condemning the fleeting expletives ban, on the ground that it is "arbitrary and capricious," in violation of federal administrative law. The court found that the FCC's indecency regime, with fines of $325,000 for a single incident, has an especially chilling effect on documentaries and other programming produced by nonprofit and community radio and TV stations.[1]

But in 2009, the Supreme Court reversed that decision, ruling that the FCC's new "fleeting expletives" rule is not arbitrary and capricious. The justices sent the case back to the Second Circuit to decide whether the FCC's current indecency policy violates the First Amendment.[2]

Judging from the tenor of today's oral argument, there is little doubt that the Second Circuit will once again rule against the FCC, this time on constitutional, not administrative law, grounds. As Judge Leval said, the agency's current censorship regime is characterized by "bewildering vagueness," resulting in a chill on free speech "vastly beyond anything contemplated in *Pacifica*"—the 1978 case in which the Supreme Court, by a narrow 5-4 vote, first approved the FCC's indecency standard.[3]

Judge Leval asked FCC lawyer Jacob Lewis whether the producer of a program in which two experts debate the pros and cons of virginity until marriage can feel sure that no indecency fine will result. "I suspect you can," Lewis answered. Leval retorted: "You suspect I can—that's very reassuring. That's the best you can say because there's no way of telling."

Lewis disagreed, pointing to "prior decisions of the Commission" allowing this sort of discussion. Judge Pooler then interjected: "You know what a good lawyer would say? If in doubt, don't run it, and that's the problem." That is, the FCC's broad and subjective censorship policies produce a chilling effect on free speech because prudent broadcasters, advised by cautious lawyers, won't take a chance.

This case will soon be back at the Supreme Court, unless the FCC decides not to appeal the probable Second Circuit ruling against it, and instead reverts to the less censorious, though equally vague, policy it followed, more or less, since about 1987: making a "contextual" judgment about what is indecent, and not punishing mere "fleeting expletives." Although unlikely, such a decision by the Obama Administration could be prudent, because once the case is back at the Supreme Court, the networks as well as the free expression and arts communities will surely argue that the entire indecency regime should be scrapped.

Such arguments would be compelling. Broadcasting is no longer the "uniquely pervasive" medium it was when the Supreme Court decided *Pacifica*: today, cable TV and the Internet have full First Amendment protection; and it is strangely anomalous that a government agency should still be allowed to punish "indecent" but constitutionally protected speech in broadcasting. Moreover, the availability of parental control devices like the v-chip undermines the child-protection rationale given in *Pacifica* for the FCC's power to censor. As Justice Ruth Bader Ginsburg wrote in the first Supreme Court round of this case, "there is no way to hide the long shadow the First Amendment casts over what the Commission has done."[4]

January 13, 2010

**Update:** The optimistic hopes expressed in the paragraph above, engendered no doubt by the keen perceptions of the court of appeals judges at the oral argument, turned out to be unrealized. On July 13, 2010, the court of appeals did indeed rule that the FCC's indecency policy is unconstitutionally vague, thereby failing to put broadcasters on notice of what is banned, and chilling free expression.[5] But on June 21, 2012, the Supreme Court ended this prolonged litigation not with a bang but a whimper: it vacated the court of appeals decision, avoided the First Amendment issues, and voided the FCC's orders only on the narrow technical ground that the agency had not given the networks fair notice of its new "fleeting expletives" rule.[6]

Thus, the strangely antiquated FCC censorship regime continues. As of 2018, it is not clear if the expletive-laden speech of the nation's president will inspire the agency to relax its rule against fleeting expletives on the airwaves.

## Notes

1. *Fox Television Stations v. FCC*, 489 F. 3d 444 (2d Cir. 2007).

2. *FCC v. Fox Television Stations*, 556 U.S. 502, 129 S.Ct. 1800 (2009).

3. *FCC v. Pacifica Foundation*, 438 U.S. 726 (1978).

4. *FCC v. Fox Television Stations*, 129 S. Ct. at 1828 (dissent by Justice Ginsburg).

5. *Fox Television Stations v. FCC*, 613 F. 3d 317 (2d Cir. 2010).

6. *FCC v. Fox Television Stations*, 132 S. Ct. 2307 (2012).

# Why Nine Court Defeats Haven't Stopped States From Trying to Restrict Violent Video Games

The August 6, 2007 decision by U.S. District Judge Ronald Whyte striking down California's video game censorship law was the ninth such ruling by a federal court in the past six years. Yet state and local legislators continue to press for laws restricting minors' access to games with "violence," "inappropriate violence," "ultra violence," or whatever other term they hope will ban the games they think harmful.

According to the Web site Game Censorship.com, Delaware, Indiana, Kansas, New York, North Carolina, and Utah are currently considering legislation restricting minors' access to games with violent content. The nine states or localities whose laws have been struck down include (in addition to California) Indianapolis, St. Louis, Michigan, Washington, Illinois, Louisiana, Minnesota, and Oklahoma.[1]

Why do lawmakers continue to press for censorship of video games despite the clear unconstitutionality of the enterprise? The answer probably lies in the long history of media violence politics, a history that goes back more than a century, to an era when concerns that crime and detective magazines would corrupt urban youth first led to laws banning stories of "bloodshed, lust, or crime." The concern resurfaced in the 1930s, once movies captured the national imagination, and again in the 1950s when television became our dominant mass medium, while crime-and-adventure comics were accused of causing juvenile delinquency. In the 1960s, '70s, and '80s, the government liberally funded researchers who sought to prove harmful effects from gunslinger shows and other televised violence, and politicians as well as the researchers often misrepresented the dubious results of their experiments.[2]

Fast forward to 2000, when four professional associations issued a "Joint Statement" asserting that "well over 1,000 studies ... point overwhelmingly to a causal connection between media violence and aggressive behavior in some children." The Statement was so rife with errors that it was difficult to understand how these groups—which included the American Medical Association (the AMA)—could have endorsed it.[3]

Dr. Edward Hill, chair-elect of the AMA, shed considerable light on this question the following year during a panel discussion. Responding to questions about the Joint Statement, Dr. Hill frankly explained that it was the AMA's desire for health education funding that drove its support of the Joint Statement. The AMA is "sometimes used by the politicians," he said. "We try to balance that because we try to use them also, so it's a contest. ... There were political reasons for signing on. We're looking for a champion in Congress that will be willing to back our desire for funding for comprehensive school health in this country."[4]

By the late 1990s, violent video games were stirring new concerns. Their interactivity, some critics said, increased the risk of imitative behavior. Psychologist Craig Anderson became a prominent spokesman for this view; among his experimental findings were that subjects who had played violent games in a laboratory administered slightly longer "noise blasts" than a control group. They also recognized "aggressive words" slightly more quickly. (The difference was in fractions of a second.) Anderson posited that recognizing aggressive words reflects aggressive thoughts, and that aggressive thoughts lead to aggressive behavior.[5]

Anderson's research was certainly squishy, but several states and localities relied on it between 2000 and 2006 in passing laws to restrict minors' access to video games. St. Louis's ordinance, for example, criminalized selling, renting, or otherwise making available to minors any "graphically violent" video game, or permitting free play of such a game without the consent of a parent or guardian. The St. Louis County Council, before passing the law, heard testimony from Anderson that playing violent games for ten to fifteen minutes causes "aggressive behavior" and "that children have more aggressive thoughts and frequently more aggressive behavior after playing violent video games."[6]

A federal district court judge relied on these statements in upholding the law, but the Court of Appeals reversed, finding the County's conclusions to be "simply unsupported in the record." Anderson's "vague generality" about aggressive thoughts and behavior, the appellate judges wrote, "falls far short of a showing that video games are psychologically deleterious," and other testimony was equally "ambiguous, inconclusive, or irrelevant."[7]

The appellate judges in the St. Louis case cited a decision from a sister court, striking down Indianapolis's ordinance. In that case, the court observed that from Grimm's fairy tales to horror movies and epic poems, violent themes have been part of children's literature; to shield them from the subject "would not only be quixotic, but deforming." Neither Anderson's "aggressive word" and "noise blast" experiments nor any other evidence before the court showed that video games "have ever caused anyone to commit a violent act," or "have caused the average level of violence to increase anywhere."[8]

In Illinois, federal judge Matthew Kennelly was particularly skeptical of expert witness testimony from Anderson and another psychologist, William Kronenberger. Judge Kennelly noted that Anderson had acknowledged exaggerating the significance of studies that show a correlation between aggressive behavior and video game play (rather than an actual causative relationship); that the longer noise blasts his subjects gave after playing violent games were "a matter of milliseconds"; and that he had manipulated the data and methodology in his "meta-analyses." More credible, Kennelly found, were the plaintiffs' experts, who testified that Anderson "not only had failed to cite any peer-reviewed studies that had shown a definitive causal link between violent video game play and aggression, but also had ignored research that reached conflicting conclusions." The judge was equally unsparing in his dissection of Dr. Kronenberger's testimony that studies of adolescent brain activity point to harm from violent video games.[9]

None of this means, of course, that some violent media might not sometimes reinforce violent attitudes in some people, or even, occasionally, contribute to violent behavior. A lack of proof in court is simply that: a lack of proof. It doesn't mean that the contrary has been proven. Certainly, there are isolated instances of direct imitation, and certainly, the sadistic or misogynistic ideas found in some games are disturbing. As the court decisions suggest, though, it's impossible to define what kind of violent images are harmful—just as it's impossible to pinpoint or quantify violent entertainment's possibly positive effects in relieving tension or processing aggressive feelings in a safe way.

The California law was typical in its unsuccessful attempt to craft a definition of "violent video game" that wouldn't be so broad as to encompass the universe of historical, sports, fantasy, sci-fi, action/adventure, knights-in-armor, simulated battlefield, or classic literature games. The definition had two parts: it banned distribution to minors of games that either (1) enable players to inflict virtual injury "in a manner which is especially heinous, cruel, or depraved," or that (2) "appeal to a deviant or morbid interest of minors," are "patently offensive to prevailing standards in the community as to what is suitable for minors," and "lack serious literary, artistic, political, or scientific value for minors."

That latter definition was borrowed from the familiar three-part test that courts have used to condemn sexual material that's deemed "obscene" or "harmful to minors." But as Judge Whyte explained, violent expression is generally protected by the First Amendment unless the government can show a "compelling" reason for its suppression; "obscene" sexual expression is not. As for California's alternative definition ("heinous, cruel, or depraved"), he pointed out that it "has no exception for material with some redeeming value and is therefore too broad. The definition could literally apply to some classic literature if put in the form of a video game."[10]

Despite the impossibility of drafting a video game censorship law that wouldn't be unconstitutionally vague and overbroad, politics will likely continue to drive this debate—at least until health professionals, legislators, and other policymakers agree to unite behind programs of media literacy education and genuine violence reduction rather than attacking entertainment and creative expression. California's action hero turned Governor Arnold Schwarzenegger, the defendant in the California case, would be an ideal candidate to lead such an initiative.

August 15, 2007

**Update:** In 2009, the Ninth Circuit Court of Appeals affirmed Judge Whyte's ruling that the state had failed to prove its claim that violent video games cause psychological or neurological harm to minors. It found that the state's reliance on Professor Craig Anderson's study was undermined by Anderson's own disclaimers and his abandonment of an effort to link presumed psychological harm to the age of his subjects. By this point, the state had acknowledged that the part of its law targeting "especially heinous, cruel, or depraved" game content was unconstitutionally overbroad.[11]

The U.S. Supreme Court granted review and on June 27, 2011 affirmed the lower courts and struck down the California law. Antonin Scalia wrote for a majority of five justices that politicians cannot create new exceptions to the First Amendment based on the unproven assumption that the harm from certain content in entertainment outweighs the benefit. But a concurring opinion by Justices Samuel Alito and John Roberts, and a dissent by Justices Clarence Thomas and Stephen Breyer, which cited the very studies that courts have found to be flawed and meaningless, may invite those who see censorship as an answer to keep trying.[12]

**Notes**

1. See *Entertainment Software Ass'n v. Blagojevich*, 404 F. Supp. 2d 1051 (N.D. Ill. 2005), affirmed, 469 F.3d 641 (7th Cir. 2006); *Entertainment Merchants Ass'n v. Henry*, 2006 U.S. Dist. LEXIS 74186 (W.D. Okla. 2006); *Entertainment*

*Software Ass'n v. Foti*, 451 F. Supp. 2d 823 (M.D. La. 2006); *Entertainment Software Ass'n v. Granholm*, 426 F. Supp. 2d 646 (E.D. Mich. 2006); *Entertainment Software Ass'n v. Hatch*, 443 F. Supp. 2d 1065 (D. Minn. 2006); *Video Software Dealers Ass'n v. Maleng*, 325 F. Supp. 2d 1180 (W.D. Wash. 2004); *Interactive Digital Software Ass'n v. St. Louis County*, 329 F.3d 954 (8th Cir. 2003); *American Amusement Machine Ass'n v. Kendrick*, 244 F.3d 572 (7th Cir. 2001).

2.  For the historical background, see Marjorie Heins, *Not in Front of the Children: "Indecency," Censorship, and the Innocence of Youth* (2007), 47-55, 98, 233-53.

3.  American Academy of Pediatrics, American Psychological Association, American Medical Association, American Academy of Child & Adolescent Psychology, Joint Statement on the Impact of Television Violence on Children, July 26, 2000.

4.  Marjorie Heins, Letter to Dr. Edward Hill, 6/11/2002, asking whether, in view of his statements, the AMA would reconsider its position. A tape recording of the Dr. Hill's remarks (at a panel discussion in New York City sponsored by the Freedom Forum on May 1, 2001) is in the author's files. Dr. Hill never responded.

5.  Craig Anderson & Karen Dill, "Video Games and Aggressive Thoughts, Feelings, and Behavior in the Laboratory and in Life," 78(4) *Journal of Personality & Social Psych.* 772 (2000).

6.  See *Interactive Digital Software Ass'n v. St. Louis County*, 329 F.3d 954 (8th Cir. 2003); The Brief *Amici Curiae* of 33 Media Scholars in this case quotes Anderson's testimony

before the St. Louis County Council; available at http://ncac.org/fepp-articles/friend-of-the-court-brief-by-33-media-scholars-in-st-louis-video-games-censorship-case.

7.  329 F.3d at 959. The court in this case also had before it the *amicus* brief of 33 media scholars, debunking claims of scientifically proven harm (see note 6). For other sources on the "effects" research, see Jonathan Freedman, *Media Violence and Its Effect on Aggression: Assessing the Scientific Evidence* (2002); Karen Sternheimer, *It's Not the Media: The Truth About Pop Culture's Influence on Children* (2003); Gerard Jones, *Killing Monsters: Why Children NEED Fantasy, Super-Heroes, and Make-Believe Violence* (2002).

8.  *American Amusement Machine Ass'n v. Kendrick*, 244 F.3d 572, 577-80 (7th Cir. 2001).

9.  *Entertainment Software Ass'n v. Blagojevich*, 404 F. Supp. 2d at 1058-67.

10.  *Video Software Dealers Ass'n v. Schwarzenegger*, No. C-05-04188 RMW (N.D. Cal. Aug. 6, 2007), 13.

11.  *Video Software Dealers Ass'n v. Schwarzenegger*, 556 F.3d 950 (9th Cir. 2009).

12.  *Brown v. Entertainment Merchants Association*, 564 U.S. 786 (2011).

# What's Wrong With Censoring Youth?

## Review of *Saving Our Children From the First Amendment*, by Kevin Saunders (2003)

Law professor Kevin Saunders's new book expands the ambitious agenda of his 1996 volume, *Violence as Obscenity*. In the earlier work, Saunders proposed to outlaw art or entertainment with violent content if it is "patently offensive," lacks "serious value," and appeals to a "morbid or shameful interest in violence." His sequel urges radically diminished constitutional protection not only for violent images and ideas, but for hate speech, vulgarity, and advertising, if they are available to minors.

The courts already accord minors lesser First Amendment rights than adults, especially when the subject matter is sex, but Saunders would go farther. He argues for an across-the-board "rational basis" standard of legal review for any censorship aimed at youth, rather than the "strict scrutiny" that usually applies, and that requires a showing of a compelling state interest in repression—in this context, that the particular speech to be censored causes identifiable harm. Saunders knows that the strict scrutiny standard cannot be met for the large categories of speech that he would like to block from youthful minds. By divesting all this speech of constitutional protection whenever it is made available to minors, Saunders avoids the First Amendment strict scrutiny problem.

Saunders lumps together several quite different perceived evils in his censorship plan. Advertising properly has less First Amendment protection than art, entertainment, or speech about political matters, and its regulation is already subject to a less rigorous standard of judicial oversight than strict scrutiny. Few would quarrel with Saunders's view that government has a role in regulating advertising that is specifically directed at impressionable children (on Saturday morning cartoon shows, for example).

Racist propaganda resembles advertising in one respect: it is an unambiguous attempt to persuade, and Saunders makes a strong case that white supremacist, anti-Semitic music has the potential to convert at least some disaffected youths into virulent racists. Whether the effect is so direct and pervasive as to justify censorship, or whether a system of hate-speech censorship such as is common in Europe will really reduce racism and anti-Semitism, are separate questions. Saunders finesses them by resorting to his proposed "rational basis" standard of judicial review. In this scenario, it is unclear whether racist epithets are to be off-limits for youth; whether there would be a "serious value" defense for racist works such as D.W. Griffith's groundbreaking silent film, *Birth of a Nation*; and whether books, movies, and Web sites that deal with Holocaust denial would also be banned.

These definitional questions become even more pressing when we think about Saunders' two largest targets, violence and vulgarity. These categories of speech are harder to define for censorship purposes than advertising or racist propaganda, and their effects are more difficult to discern. In a short chapter called "The Costs of Free Expression," Saunders relies upon some of the most discredited studies in the media effects field to bolster his argument that violent imagery causes violent behavior—for example, the researcher Brandon Centerwall's conclusion in a 1992 article that since he had found a correlation between the introduction of television and a doubling in homicide rates in a particular locality, this meant that TV was responsible for the added real-world mayhem. Centerwall's claims have been thoroughly debunked.[1] In *Violence as Obscenity*, Saunders gave a more balanced description of Centerwall's work, but this nuance is dropped in the current volume.

To his credit, Saunders acknowledges critiques of the claims that have been made for proof of widespread imitative effects from media violence—including the critiques of this reviewer. He even allows that some fantasy violence may be cathartic. But then he dismisses these ambiguities by resorting to his proposed rational basis standard of legal scrutiny for censorship affecting minors. Under this standard, it does not matter what empirical evidence shows or does not show: a huge category of creative expression would be restricted because it is not irrational for policymakers to think it might be harmful.

The argument for harm becomes even more dubious when Saunders gets to vulgarity—what he calls the "coarsening of society." Here, using the term "harm" is completely misplaced. The "coarsening of society" is entirely a matter of taste, and talk of harm is a poor substitute for the real social interest that Saunders expounds: teaching minors standards of politeness and civility.

If defining the speech Saunders wants to censor turns out to be difficult, constructing the censorship apparatus is a logistical nightmare. Saunders offers a few proposals for how censorship of youth might work in a society where children are not raised in closed containers, and every effort at suppression runs the risk of reducing the adult population to reading and viewing only what is deemed appropriate for children. But his proposed censorship schemes are problematic.

For example, the Federal Communications Commission currently has the power to censor "indecency" on radio and broadcast television. Saunders would extend this and have government ban "sales to children of CDs [or videos] with offensive or indecent language." He even suggests criminalizing the language on the famous "Fuck the Draft" jacket worn by a young protester named Paul Cohen to express his opinion on the Vietnam War, if the malefactor knowingly wears the jacket in the presence of children.[2]

Our recent history suggests the danger of giving government officials the power to impose their standards of taste or decency on any speech that minors might see or hear. Their judgments are usually conservative, conventional, and dismissive of radical or minority styles, as indecency findings against Pacifica radio over the years, and more recently against the feminist rap artist Sarah Jones, make clear.[3] Like Jones's rap song "Your Revolution" and George Carlin's famous "seven dirty words" monolog, Paul Cohen's jacket was core political speech—and very relevant speech for those at or approaching draft age.

Turning to the logistics of censoring youth online, Saunders proposes an expansion of a voluntary rating scheme called "PICS" (Platform for Internet Content Selection). PICS would criminalize any Internet speech deemed inappropriate for minors (including not only sexual material but "profane language" and "Internet hate speech"), if the speaker or publisher does not "self-rate" so that the material can be electronically blocked from youthful eyes. Even apart from the chilling effect this would have on Web speakers who do not wish to self-identify as purveyors of "harmful" expression, the definitional problems remain, whether the material in question includes the raunchier parts of James Joyce's *Ulysses,* the graphic violence in *Saving Private Ryan,* George Carlin's hilarious "Filthy Words" monolog, Shakespeare's bloody *Titus Andronicus,* or countless other examples.

It is easy to make light of Saunders's proposals, with their massive definitional and logistical problems. I do not mean to do so. His sincerity is genuine, and he is responding to widespread concerns about what are probably real—if unprovable—ill effects on youth from overdoses of popular culture. But as I have argued elsewhere (see, *e.g., Not in Front of the Children*), censorship provides only symbolic relief from these concerns. It neither teaches youngsters the lessons that Saunders and many others want to teach (civility, nonviolence, racial tolerance, sexual restraint), nor helps them mature into critically thinking adults.

It remains, however, a seductive distraction from the more difficult, costly, and long-term educational approach to concerns about media effects. And, as Saunders's new book suggests, it offers attractive publishing opportunities for legal academics.

April 19, 2004

### Notes

1.  Brandon Centerwall, "Television and Violence: The Scale of the Problem and Where to Go From Here," 267(22) *J.A.M.A.* 3059 (1992). For literature debunking Centerwall, see Franklin Zimring and Gordon Hawkins,

*Crime is Not the Problem—Lethal Violence in America* (1997), 133-34, 239-43; Steven Messner, "Television Violence and Violent Crime," 33(3) *Social Problems* 218, 228 (1986); Jonathan Freedman, "Viewing Television Violence Does Not Make People More Aggressive," 22 *Hofstra Law Review.* 833, 849-51 (1994).

2. Cohen was criminally prosecuted; the Supreme Court overturned his conviction in *Cohen v. California*, 403 U.S. 15 (1971).

3. See "The Strange Case of Sarah Jones," in this volume.

# Part Three:
## The Arts

# The Notorious Women Artists of 1943

The art collector Peggy Guggenheim had just opened her avant-garde Art of This Century gallery on West 57 Street in New York City in the fall of 1942 when her friend Marcel Duchamp suggested that she mount an all-woman exhibition. Guggenheim loved the idea: the show would be radical not only because of the sex of its artists but because most of the paintings, drawings, and sculptures on view would be either abstract or Surrealist in style, as befitted Guggenheim's modernist taste.

"31 Women" attracted attention in part because one of its artists was the popular vaudeville stripper Gypsy Rose Lee, who was also a writer and a denizen of bohemian cultural circles; her contribution was a collage titled "Self-Portrait" (she was clothed). The more serious, full-time artists included the up-and-coming abstract sculptor Louise Nevelson and the Surrealists Frida Kahlo, Leonora Carrington, Leonor Fini, and Meret Oppenheim, whose work, a teacup and spoon covered in fur, had caused gasps when it was shown at the Museum of Modern Art's "Fantastic Art" exhibition seven years before.

Kahlo was already famous, in part because of her marriage to the painter Diego Rivera, who had refused to comply with John D. Rockefeller, Jr.'s demand in 1933 that Rivera remove an image of Vladimir Lenin from his mural at Rockefeller Center. (Rockefeller then had the mural destroyed.) Kahlo's contribution to "31 Women" was a pencil drawing, "Self-Portrait with Cropped Hair." Dressed severely in men's clothes, with her shorn hair on the floor around her, Kahlo's grim self-portrait was likely a response to Rivera's chronic infidelities.

Leonor Fini's contribution, a painting called "The Shepherdess of the Sphinxes," drew on classic Surrealist themes of sexuality and, in this case, female power: it depicted a scantily-clad, voluptuous shepherdess in a dream landscape filled with equally voluptuous sphinxes who seem to have been feasting on bones and flowers. (It's now at the Peggy Guggenheim Collection in Venice.) Surrealist Kay Sage's painting, "At the Appointed Time," depicted a more abstract nightmarish landscape dominated by an ominous vertical metallic pillar, a road leading nowhere, and slimy, snakelike forms crawling over two horizontal beams.

Newcomer Dorothea Tanning's "Birthday" showed a half-undressed young woman standing beside a seemingly infinite series of receding doors; a birdlike monster lies at her feet. Tanning's work was chosen by the celebrated European Surrealist, Max Ernst, then married to Guggenheim; she had assigned him the task of visiting the studios of promising female artists in order to choose likely candidates for the upcoming show. Ernst, a notorious womanizer, promptly left Guggenheim and moved in with the much younger Tanning.

Georgia O'Keeffe declined an invitation to participate in the show, saying that she refused to be categorized as a "woman painter." She could afford to be particular, having by this time attained substantial recognition on her own, thanks in part to the male-dominated art establishment's highly sexualized interpretation of her mystical abstractions. (O'Keeffe always denied any sexual symbolism in her work.)

Other female artists did not have O'Keeffe's ability to pick and choose their venues: several, like the sculptor Xenia Cage, labored under the shadows of their more famous husbands (in her case, the composer John Cage); others, like the painter

Buffie Johnson, knew plenty about sex discrimination in the art world: the *Time* magazine critic James Stern had bluntly refused her request that he review the show, observing that women should stick to having babies.[1]

Those critics who did review "31 Women" greeted it with a mixture of grudging admiration and dismissive condescension. *The New York Times* reviewer, Edward Alden Jewell, damned the show with faint praise and a patronizing tone. First, he made fun of the unconventionally undulating walls and biomorphic furniture in Guggenheim's gallery; then he mocked Louise Nevelson's "Column" ("you would call it sculpture, I guess," he wrote). But he did note that "the exhibition yields one captivating surprise after another."[2]

"H.B.," the critic for *Art Digest*, wrote in a similar vein: "Now that women are becoming serious about Surrealism, there is no telling where it will all end. An example of them exposing their subconscious may be viewed with alarm at the Art of the Century headquarters during January."[3]

The worst of the put-downs came from Henry McBride in the *New York Sun*: women Surrealists were actually better than men, he said, because after all, "Surrealism is about 70% hysterics, 20% literature, 5% good painting and 5% just saying boo to the innocent public. There are, as we all know, plenty of men among the New York neurotics but we also know that there are still more women among them. Considering the statistics the doctors hand out, and considering the percentages listed above, ... it is obvious women ought to excel at Surrealism."[4]

A final critic, in *Art News*, likewise could not resist snarky asides, but also raised serious questions about the wisdom of mounting woman-only shows. "Division of the sexes, or rather segregation of the female of the species, is ordinarily a dubious policy for an art show," the anonymous R.F. wrote; "but this time, however, there is no outbreak of watercolor or flower paintings. The women—they could never be laughingly referred to as ladies—present a chinkless armored front."[5] Women artists in 1943 evidently were damned either way, whether for creating presumably unimportant watercolors and flowers, or for being Amazons.

The condescending rhetoric of the reviewers in 1943 is largely out-of-date today, but the problem of underrepresentation of women in major art collections remains. On a recent day (in January 2016), I counted the works by female artists on the walls of the Metropolitan Museum of Art's Modern and Contemporary Art galleries. There were twenty-nine—as opposed to 305 works by men. That's 9.5%—up from the less-than-5% total reported by the activist group Guerrilla Girls in 1989. Still, it's not very many.

Buffie Johnson was sufficiently incensed by the sexism of the *Time* critic who thought women should stick to having babies that she wrote an article on women artists of the past, and the often insurmountable hurdles they faced. She could not find a publisher for it until 1997, when the Jackson Pollock-Lee Krasner House in East Hampton, Long Island mounted a show commemorating Guggenheim's "31 Women" as well as a second, 1945 all-woman exhibit at Guggenheim's gallery. The catalog that accompanied the Pollock-Krasner House show included Johnson's article.[6]

Buffie Johnson's contribution to the "31 Women" show in 1943, incidentally, was a painting called *"Dejeuner sur mer,"* a seascape with two women clinging to a wreck.

Other artists represented in "31 Women" were Djuna Barnes, Irene Rice Pereira, Hedda Sterne, Sophie Taeuber-Arp, Hazel McKinley, Pegeen Vail, Barbara Reis, Valentine Hugo, Jacqueline Lamba, Suzy Frelinghuysen, Esphyr Slobodkina, Maria Helena Vieira da Silva, Aline Meyer Liebman, Elsa von Freytag-Loringhoven, Julia Thecla, Sonia Secula, Gretchen Schoeninger, Elizabeth Eyre de Lanux, Meraud Guevara, Anne Harvey, and Milena Pavlović Barili, who is not well-known around the world but is a hero in her native Serbia: several of her works have been reproduced on Yugoslavian postage stamps.

March 2016

An earlier version of this article, which includes reproductions of several of the paintings mentioned here, was published on the Web site of the Gotham Center For New York City History, https://www.gothamcenter.org/blog/the-notorious-31-women-art-show-of-1943.

## Notes

1.  As recounted in Buffie Johnson, "Women in Art: The Embattled Woman Artist," in Siobhán Conaty, *Art of This Century: The Women* (Pollock-Krasner House, 1999).

2.  Edward Alden Jewell, "31 Women Artists Show Their Work," *NY Times*, 1/8/43, 23.

3.  H.B., "Feminine Surrealists," *Art Digest*, 1/15/43, 15.

4.  Henry McBride, "Women Surrealists," *New York Sun*, 1/18/43, quoted in *Peggy Guggenheim and Frederick Kiesler:*

*The Story of Art of this Century* (Susan Davidson and Philip Rylands, eds., 2004), 292.

5. R.F., "31 Odd Women at Peggy Guggenheim's," *Art News*, 2/1/43, 20.

6. See note 1, above.

Other sources: EXHIBITION BY 31 WOMEN (exhibition announcement) (Art of This Century, Jan. 1943); Whitney Chadwick, *Women Artists & the Surrealist Movement* (1985); and the Sugswriters Blog, which, as of 2017, contained biographies of all 31 of the women: http://sugswritersblog.blogspot.com.

# *Harvard Law Review* Censors Link to a Nan Goldin Photograph—In a Forum Celebrating Free Expression, No Less

The *Harvard Law Review* has censored a link to an image by the prominent photographer Nan Goldin, ostensibly because of concerns about child pornography. The image, "Klara and Eddy Belly Dancing," shows two little girls cavorting, one of them nude. The link was included in my article, "The Brave New World of Social Media Censorship," which discusses censorship by private companies that offer social-media sites, web hosting, and browsing services.

All this began after I was invited to comment on a paper to be presented at a day-long symposium at Harvard Law School celebrating the fiftieth anniversary of a major Supreme Court First Amendment decision, *New York Times Co. v. Sullivan.*[1] At the conference, held in February 2014, I delivered my comments, which were later to be published in the *Law Review's* online Forum. At some point in the publication process, an editor asked me to delete a reference to an incident in which a Web hosting company expelled the National Coalition Against Censorship (NCAC) from its servers because of the presence of the Goldin photograph. The editor told me that a link to the image could be "troubling" to some readers. I declined to delete the reference, and reminded the editor that this was, after all, a symposium celebrating freedom of expression.

Subsequently, the *Review's* editor-in-chief called, and told me somewhat apologetically that the *Review* had consulted its outside counsel at the Boston law firm of Ropes and Gray, who advised against publishing the link. Despite the questionable nature of the legal advice, I realized (as I told the apologetic editor) that the *Review* had painted itself into a corner, and I acquiesced in its deletion of the link while retaining my description of the original censorship incident. I added a note reporting that a link to the photograph on the NCAC Web site was deleted, "over the strenuous objection of the author, on the advice of counsel for the *Harvard Law Review*," and deploring the *Review's* concern about "a link to an innocent photograph by one of the country's major artists" as "evidence of both the danger and the absurdity of confusing images of children's bodies with child pornography."[2]

June 26, 2014

---

"Klara and Eddy Belly Dancing" can be found at http://www.thefileroom.org/documents/dyn/DisplayCase.cfm/id/1310, or just by googling the title.

An earlier version of this article is available at http://ncac.org/fepp-articles/harvard-law-review-censors-link-to-nan-goldin-photograph.

## Notes

1. 376 U.S. 254 (1964). *New York Times v. Sullivan* was a landmark not only for freedom of speech but for the civil rights movement. The city commissioner of Montgomery, Alabama, sued the *Times* for libel on account of an ad placed by civil rights groups supporting the desegregation efforts of Martin Luther King, Jr. and others; the ad contained minor factual errors. An Alabama jury awarded damages of $500,000. The

Supreme Court reversed the judgment, ruling that given the First Amendment interest in political debate that is "uninhibited, robust, and wide-open," a public official, to recover damages in a libel case, must prove not only that false statements were made that harmed his reputation, but that the defendant who published them had actual knowledge of their falsity, or else a reckless disregard for their truth or falsity.

2. Marjorie Heins, "The Brave New World of Social Media Censorship," *Harvard Law Review Forum*, 6/20/2014, n.8, https://harvardlawreview.org/2014/06/the-brave-new-world-of-social-media-censorship/.

# Words on Fire: Book Censorship in America

This essay is slightly modified from a presentation to the conference Words on Fire: The Bonfires of Berlin: How It Happened Then—Why It Matters Now, Boston, March 2003.

It is a bit daunting to be asked to talk about book censorship in the U.S. at an event devoted primarily to remembering the book burnings of Nazi Germany. We occasionally have book burnings here, organized by private groups like the Christ Community Church in Alamogordo, New Mexico, which burned J.K. Rowling's Harry Potter books along with works by William Shakespeare in January 2002, claiming that they were "satanic deceptions."[1] But these incidents are relatively infrequent, and are not, as in Nazi Germany, conducted with the approval and encouragement of the government and orchestrated by the nation's major university student association.

Nevertheless, we do have book censorship in the U.S. Let me give you a quick background on American censorship history, followed by an outline of the problems we face today with attacks on books in public schools and libraries.

Book censorship of course has a long history predating the horrors of Nazi Germany. Until the Enlightenment in the eighteenth century, virtually all governments and powerful churches, with rare exceptions, suppressed words and ideas they considered threatening to their hegemony— which meant, for the most part, words and ideas thought to be subversive or blasphemous. By contrast, America in the mid-nineteenth century, taking its cue from England, began the official suppression of books and ideas not about politics or religion but about sexuality—which is itself, of course, a political subject, because the targets were ideas and information that threatened dominant attitudes about women's role, about reproduction, and about social control of sexual behavior.

This new form of official government censorship was accomplished through the passage of laws against "obscenity." Three social factors combined to produce our first obscenity laws:

- Victorian-era official morality, in particular, attitudes about women's sexual nature or lack thereof;

- Fear that a newly literate working class would be corrupted by novels, detective stories, and other popular literature; and

- A drive by leaders of the middle and upper classes to institutionalize and control sexuality, especially birth control and abortion information, which were seen as threatening the institution of marriage and facilitating sex for pleasure rather than procreation.

All three of these factors were part of a larger political struggle. The Victorian era was not all button-down prudery; theories of free love and information about female sexuality thrived through much of the nineteenth century, and obscenity law was used to repress them. In Massachusetts, for example, the free-love radical Ezra Heywood was convicted under state obscenity law and sentenced to two years in Dedham jail for publishing a political tract called *Cupid's Yokes*, which attacked the institution of marriage.[2]

In addition to state obscenity prosecutions such as Heywood's, the federal obscenity law, named after America's most famous moral entrepreneur, Anthony Comstock, greatly expanded the scope of censorship. The U.S. had federal obscenity legislation before Comstock, but he lobbied for a major expansion in 1873, and this "Comstock Act" is still on the books. It specifically added birth control information and devices to the list of banned materials.

As head of the New York Society for the Suppression of Vice and a special agent of the U.S. Post Office as well as the New York State prosecutor's office, Comstock was able to seize and destroy tons of books, magazines, pamphlets, advertisements, and birth control devices. And although one basis of obscenity law—fear of sexual arousal—applied to everyone, youth were a particular subject of concern. The U.S. Patent Office received numerous applications for anti-masturbation devices which parents were persuaded to acquire to prevent children from falling into dreadful habits.

As Comstock wrote in one of his several books, called *Traps for the Young*: there is "no more active agent employed by Satan in civilized communities to ruin the human family than EVIL READING." Comstock's counterpart in Boston, the Watch and Ward Society, was equally unrelenting: its annual report in 1893 warned that "even the briefest of stimulating passages" in literature "could plunge the helpless reader into that state of excitement in which principle is overcome by passion and nothing but opportunity is wanted for unbridled indulgence."[3]

The legacy of these anti-vice crusaders persisted well into the twentieth century. Works suppressed under state obscenity laws, or banned from importation by Customs, or from the U.S. mails, included Boccaccio's *Decameron*, Tolstoy's *Kreutzer Sonata*, Hemingway's *For Whom the Bell Tolls*, Balzac's

*Droll Stories*, Dreiser's *An American Tragedy* (the subject of a major censorship case in Massachusetts in 1927), Edmund Wilson's *Memoirs of Hecate County*, *The Arabian Nights*, D.H. Lawrence's *Lady Chatterley's Lover* (of course), Henry Miller's *Tropic of Cancer*, James Joyce's *Ulysses*, and hundreds more. In defense of Dreiser, by the way, Massachusetts anti-censorship forces staged a free-speech rally, complete with satiric skits, while the trial was in progress. Margaret Sanger, the birth control pioneer who had been forbidden to speak in Boston, sat on the stage with a large piece of tape across her mouth.[4]

It wasn't until 1957 that the Supreme Court put any First Amendment limits on obscenity law, announcing that if literature had redeeming social value, it could not be suppressed. The first unexpurgated *Lady Chatterley* followed, and by the late 1960s, even *Fanny Hill* was protected—according to the Supreme Court, because it has literary and historical value. The case was a turning point for the Court, which had been struggling to come up with a definition of "obscenity" that would recognize both the importance to a free society of protecting literature and information about human sexuality, and the apparent political necessity of having laws in place to censor sexual material that—in the Court's words—lacks "serious value" and is "no essential part of the exposition of ideas."[5]

Today in the U.S., books are not suppressed very often through the criminal prohibitions of obscenity law. But they are the subject of unending censorship battles in public schools and libraries—and here, the targets of disapproval include unconventional religious beliefs, radical politics, violent imagery, magic, vulgar words, and disobedience of authority—in addition, of course, to sex. Sometimes these battles are national in scope, as, for example, when Congress passed a law called "CIPA" (Children's Internet Protection Act) in 2000, which required most American schools and libraries to install privately manufactured Internet filters that block tens of thousands of valuable Web pages, including many that have nothing to do with sex. The subjects that were blocked by some filters ranged from fly fishing to the Knights of Columbus. A federal district court invalidated the law, finding that Internet filters are crude mechanisms that go way beyond any legitimate purpose of protecting children; but the Supreme Court reversed.[6]

More frequently, censorship of school curriculum and library books are not imposed by Congress but by local school boards. This is a result in part of our decentralized educational system, which allows relatively small but highly vocal and determined local pressure groups to influence school boards and administrators. Most challenges come from the religious right, but those leaning politically left are hardly immune to the impulse to suppress what they think—whether or not correctly—is dangerous literature. In the context of school censorship, *Huckleberry Finn* is probably the best example. In 2002, this masterpiece ranked seventh in the nation on the American Library Association's annual tally of most challenged books.[7]

The first six books on the list were the Harry Potter series, for its focus on wizardry and magic; the *Alice* series, for sexual explicitness and offensive language; Robert Cormier's *The Chocolate War*, for offensive language; Maya Angelou's *I Know Why the Caged Bird Sings*, for sexual content, alleged racism, and offensive language (the alleged racism is usually described as an unfair depiction of white people); *Taming the Star Runner* by S.E. Hinton, for offensive language; and Dav Pilkey's *Captain Underpants* series, for "encouraging children to disobey authority."[8]

Campaigns to remove books from school curricula and libraries go back decades. In one incident in 1975, seven members of the school board in a Long Island, New York town called Island Trees ordered the removal from school libraries of nine books that had been listed as "objectionable" by a local conservative group. They included Kurt Vonnegut's *Slaughterhouse Five*, Piri Thomas's *Down These Mean Streets*, Desmond Morris's *The Naked Ape*, and *Best Short Stories* by Negro Writers, edited by Langston Hughes. The school board members explained that they had been told the books were "anti-American, anti-Christian, anti-Semitic, and just plain filthy."[9] Unlike many similar school censorship incidents, this one ended up at the Supreme Court, largely thanks to a student named Steven Pico who sued the school district, alleging violation of his First Amendment rights.

The Supreme Court eventually issued what we call a compromise decision in Pico's case. On the one hand, it said school boards have broad discretion to select or remove books that they consider "pervasively vulgar." But on the other hand, a narrow majority of five justices said that some motivations for the removal of books from school libraries would violate the First Amendment—in particular, motivations that are based on disapproval of a particular viewpoint. Three justices joined in an opinion explaining that school boards may not act "in a narrowly partisan or political manner," because "our Constitution does not permit the official suppression of ideas."[10] Two other justices joined in the judgment, to create the majority of five.

This *Pico* standard—prohibiting book removal decisions that are aimed at the "suppression of ideas"—still generally governs in school censorship cases; as a result, most school boards have learned to articulate justifications for their removal decisions in terms of "vulgarity," "inappropriate content," or age suitability, rather than hostility to particular points of view.

Thus, for example, a perennial target of local school censors, Steinbeck's *Of Mice and Men*, is usually challenged for vulgar language or "taking the Lord's name in vain." The book is a popular choice of high school English teachers precisely because, as one scholar has said, it is "wonderfully teachable ... : simple and clear, yet profound and beautiful." It can "show beginning readers the paths to great books. ... It is a tragedy in the classic sense, showing humanity's ability to achieve nobility through and in spite of defeat."[11]

And although *Of Mice and Men* is often challenged, the challenges don't always succeed. In Ohio in 1992, for example, after a pressure group in one town counted 108 profanities, twelve racial slurs, and forty-five uses of God's name in vain in the book and forced its removal from the local school's optional reading list, about 150 protesting parents, teachers, and students attended a review committee meeting where they extolled the book's virtues. *Of Mice and Men* was reinstated on the reading list.[12]

Let me recount just two more examples from the hundreds of book censorship incidents that occur every year. In 2002, the school board of Fairfax County, Virginia, voted to retain a historical novel for young readers, *Gates of Fire*, over the objection of a local group called PABBIS (Parents Against Bad Books), which protested its "profanity, violence, and lurid depictions of sadistic behavior." The historical setting of the book is ancient Greece, and the violence that so shocked PABBIS occurs during the Battle of Thermopylae in 480 B.C. Local free-speech advocates formed a Right to Read Coalition that persuaded the school board to retain the book.[13]

Finally, a very current case: Harry Potter again, this time in Arkansas. All Harry Potter books were removed from school library shelves in the town of Cedarville after the school board decided that they show "good witches" and "good magic," and teach that "parents/teachers/rules are stupid and something to be ignored."[14] This was despite the recommendation of a review committee that voted 15-0 to keep the books. The school board's decision was challenged in court, relying on the standard announced by the Supreme Court in the *Pico* case, since the school board removed the Harry Potter books specifically because it objected to their ideas: favorable depictions of witches, the occult, and the notion of kids challenging authority. In April 2003, a federal judge in Little Rock ordered the Cedarville School District to return the Harry Potter books to the open shelves of its libraries.[15]

An occasional loss in court, of course, will not stop other school boards from removing books from library shelves or curriculum reading lists. Book censorship will continue wherever the perennial human urge to censor trumps appreciation for the judgments of educators and the intellectual freedom of students. This is why today's Words on Fire festival is important, and why I hope it will inspire you to get active in your local freedom to read committee, or if it doesn't exist, to create one.

March 13, 2003

# Notes

1. Associated Press, "N.M. pastor leads flock in 'Potter' book burning," *Deseret News*, 12/31/2001, https://www.deseretnews.com/article/886981/NM-pastor-leads-flock-in-Potter-book-burning.html.

2. The material in this and the following paragraphs is from Marjorie Heins, *Not in Front of the Children: "Indecency," Censorship, and the Innocence of Youth* (2007).

3. *Id.*, 30.

4. *Id.*, 42.

5. *Roth v. United States*, 354 U.S. 476 (1957); *Miller v. California*, 413 U.S. 15, 24 (1973). *The Fanny Hill* case is *A Book Named John Cleland's Memoirs of a Woman of Pleasure v. Massachusetts*, 383 U.S. 413 (1966).

6. *United States v. American Library Association*, 539 U.S. 194 (2003).

7. American Library Association press release, "Harry Potter Series Tops List of Most Challenged Books Four Years in a Row," 1/13/2003, http://www.ala.org/Template.cfm?Section=Press_Releases&template=/contentmanagement/contentdisplay.cfm&ContentID=9404.

8. *Id.*

9. *Board of Education, Island Trees Union Free School District v. Pico*, 457 U.S. 853, 857 (1982).

10. *Id.*, 870. Justice William Brennan wrote the lead opinion, in which Justices Thurgood Marshall and John Paul Stevens joined. Justices Byron White and Harry

Blackmun concurred in the judgment without agreeing with all of Brennan's reasoning.

11. University of Wisconsin Professor Thomas Scarseth, quoted in Herbert Foerstel, *Banned in the USA* (1994), 143.

12. *Id.*, 145-46.

13. Reported in American Library Association, *Newsletter on Intellectual Freedom*, July 2002, 179.

14. Free Expression Network Newswire, "National Groups Urge Court to Overturn Harry Potter Ban," 3/3/2003.

15. American United for Separation of Church and State, "Federal Court Foils Arkansas School's Effort to Restrict Harry Potter," *Church and State Magazine*, June 2003, https://www.au.org/church-state/june-2003-church-state/people-events/federal-court-foils-arkansas-schools-effort-to.

# Corseted, Cosseted, and Sexually Deprived

## Review of *The Family Shakespeare* by David Stallings

It is always risky to create a work of art with an unambiguous message, and an anti-censorship message is no exception. Ambiguity, irony, and multiple meanings are the stuff of good art; an unambiguous message, no matter how right or passionate, risks sliding into agit-prop.

Playwright David Stallings's *The Family Shakespeare*, which recently opened at the June Havoc Theater in Manhattan, avoids this trap. It comes down decisively on the side of freedom, but also gives Thomas Bowdler, famous for his early nineteenth century expurgated versions of Shakespeare's plays, a chance to make his case. And its imagined riff on Thomas's sister Henrietta as champion of the uncensored life clearly exposes the perils of the more unbuttoned approach to risky ideas: charming though she is, Henrietta is also reckless, and mendacious when it suits her. Her flights of unrepressed fantasy in the play have some unfortunate results.

The historical Henrietta was not the rebel of Stallings's imagining. She was in fact the first in the family to have published some of Shakespeare's plays purged, as she put it, of "anything that can raise a blush on the cheek of modesty."[1] But as Stallings explains in his program note, "because this is a fiction I chose to take this historic family and write them with strong literary license. I chose to go beneath the black and white of research and infuse gray. Because only with the color gray do we have art."[2]

Stallings and his director, Antonio Miniño, weave deliciously appropriate quotations from Shakespeare's plays and poetry into the melodrama of their imagined Bowdler family. The two brothers and two sisters argue over morality in both life and art: in Stallings's rendering, brother John is a serial seducer of servant girls; brother Thomas is a prude; sister Jane a hypochondriac; and sister Henrietta is the most intelligent and free-spirited of the brood. Henrietta gets the good lines opposing the censorship that her beloved but stuffy brother Thomas advances. "Oh Thomas," she says after he is shocked by her use of the word "castrate":

> A child on a farm knows what castration is. A youth with a dog knows what intercourse is. And they should be able to open a book and see that the life they know is there. Or else why would people read? People will not know how to relate to the beauty in the poetry if it is not brutal and honest and true. Even a child can detect the dishonesty in censured reality.

But Thomas, earlier in the play, has argued his case for change and abridgment—what we today might call fair use. He has arrived in the family manse from London, where he has just seen the celebrated actor David Garrick in *Othello*. Garrick has over his career not only made many "prunings, transpositions, or other alterations"[3] in Shakespeare's plays; in this case, he has changed the title to "Iago." Henrietta objects:

"Thomas, it's 'Othello.'"

Thomas: He called it "Iago."

Henrietta: Why?

Thomas: Because he was playing Iago.

Henrietta: That's not a reason.

Thomas: He seemed to think it was.

Henrietta: The play is not his.

Thomas: It isn't yours either.

Thomas's argument, essentially, is that Shakespeare belongs to all of us, to modify as we choose. As the real Henrietta wrote in defense of her enterprise, "there are many editions of Shakespeare, 'with all his imperfections on his head,'"[4] and the real Thomas later added:

> The great objection which has been urged against *The Family Shakespeare*, and it has been urged with vehemence by those who have not examined the work, is the apprehension, that, with erasure of the indecent passages, the spirit and fire of the poet would often be much injured, and sometimes be entirely destroyed. This objection arises principally from those persons who have confined their study of Shakespeare to the closet, and have not learned in the theatre, with how much safety it is possible to make the necessary alterations.[5]

A fair point, especially for theater aficionados. What most troubles Stallings, in fact, is not the Bowdlers' expurgations of "the obvious swear words," but their censorship of the "gray adult colors of intent and comprehension": the Shakespearean speeches "questioning God, questioning mankind, questioning ideas that in the Bowdlers' home should never be questioned in front of women and children."[6] It is this suppression of ideas, not just sexually explicit scenes or words, that gives the verb "bowdlerize" its full resonance today.

The impulse to censor is human and universal; only the words and ideas considered dangerous have changed in the two centuries since the Bowdlers did their snipping and pruning. There is no such thing as absolute freedom of speech—think of the exceptions for defamation, invasion of privacy, threats of violence, blackmail, commercial fraud, and incitement to crime—so why not bowdlerization?

The difference is that in the realm of art and literature, the very ambiguity and multiplicity of meanings make it difficult to agree on what is dangerous or harmful. As Stallings puts it, "only with the color gray do we have art." It is almost impossible to identify predictable and tangible harm from exposure to art; people's—including children's—reactions are too variable. Falsely shouting fire in a theater is likely to cause a panic because most people will react in the same way.[7] Delineating extreme violence or sexual raunchiness in a painting, a play, a comic book, or a video game will not have such a readily predictable and uniform effect.

The *Family Shakespeare* tackles issues beyond literary censorship. Henrietta stands not just for creative freedom but for breaking the bonds of womanhood, nineteenth century-style: corseted, cosseted, and sexually deprived. She does not do much about the last of these plagues, as far as we can tell, but she does forge a sort of erotically charged sisterhood with a young woman who arrives in the household as a servant and manages to surmount multiple forms of oppression, both economic and sexual. The play ends with the two of them trading verses from Shakespeare's Sonnet 66, which contains a long list of complaints about the injustices of life, including "art made tongue-tied by authority/and folly, doctor-like, controlling skill."

Stallings has deftly chosen these and many other gems to enrich his script; what better collaborator for a playwright, after all, than Shakespeare? I don't think the family drama in the play is wholly successful, but there is more than enough wit and erudition to move things along, and much food for thought in the Henrietta-Thomas debate.

April 23, 2011

## Notes

1.  Henrietta Bowdler, Preface to *The Family Shakespeare* (1st ed. 1807), quoted in Colin Franklin, *The Bowdlers and Their Family Shakespeare* (2000).

2.  "A note from playwright David Stallings," MTWorks, *The Family Shakespeare*, April 13-30, 2011.

3.  Francis Gentleman, a colleague of Garrick's, in 1774, quoted in Colin Franklin, *supra*.

4.  Preface to *The Family Shakespeare*, *supra*, quoted in Colin Franklin, *supra*. The reference is to *Hamlet*, Act I, scene 5.

5.  Thomas Bowdler, Preface to *The Family Shakespeare* (4th ed.), quoted in Colin Franklin, *supra*.

6.  "A note from playwright David Stallings," *supra*.

7.  The famous "falsely shouting fire" example of unprotected speech was the invention of Justice Oliver Wendell Holmes, Jr., in *Schenck v. United States*, 249 U.S. 47 (1919).

# The Implications and Complications of Musical Art and Politics

## Review of *The Rest is Noise: Listening to the Twentieth Century*, by Alex Ross (2007)

Most reviews of Alex Ross's *The Rest is Noise*, a history of twentieth century Western music (for the most part, "serious" or "classical" music) have been admiring if not ecstatic, though few have turned on the theme of politics and art that threads through the central section of the book. Indeed, Ross may not have intended the theme to be so prominent: the word "censorship" is not even in the index.

Yet from the Nazi thugs who shut down the Bertolt Brecht-Kurt Weill opera, *The Rise and Fall of the City of Mahagonny*, in 1930 to Josef Stalin's stony displeasure with what he deemed decadent musical composition and subject matter in Shostakovich's *Lady Macbeth of Mtsensk* in the U.S.S.R. six years later, the control of artistic expression—in this case, music—by the totalitarian regimes that dominated the middle years of the twentieth century in Europe forms a powerful motif in Ross's text.

Add to this the far more subtle and less vicious market censorship in the Western democracies, Franklin Delano Roosevelt's sponsorship of Hollywood propaganda films during World War II, post-war McCarthy Era attacks on leftist musicians, and the sobering picture of Adolf Hitler gushing over Beethoven, Bruckner, and Wagner and using their music to bolster the drama and excitement of his psychopathic Nazi regime, and one's head is left spinning from the implications and complications of musical art and politics.

In fact, for this reader, Ross's tome loses much of its narrative drive once politics are left behind: the last few chapters recount one avant-garde experiment after another in the 1960s, '70s, '80s, and '90s, without any strong unifying theme.

But there's much food for thought in the central part of the book. One wonders if the acquiescence—if not enthusiastic support—on the part of so many German composers for Hitler was the product of moral cowardice, sickening evil, or just too-human nature. ("Thank God," Ross quotes Richard Strauss after Hitler came to power. "Finally a Reich Chancellor who is interested in art" (305)). What made some artists resist or flee, and others become collaborators in the Nazi horrors?

Similarly, in Stalinist Russia, why did Shostakovich refuse to defect to the West—and instead, indulge in numerous abject confessions of counter-revolutionary tendencies, while his colleagues were being jailed and murdered, and he was threatened with a similar fate? And what did the European exiles from Hitler lose—and what gain—from their move to America, often to Hollywood, where they wrote movie soundtracks or obtained teaching jobs at the nation's expanding Cold War universities?

Although Ross offers no answers to these questions, he amply demonstrates the interconnection of art, including musical art, and politics. "Art for art's sake" has little mention here. From Aaron Copland's involvement in the leftist Popular Front of the '30s to early radio companies' eagerness to demonstrate that the medium was operating in the public interest by broadcasting classical music, Ross shows how culture is shaped by political circumstance, even where no commissar of musical correctness is in place.

He also shows how music, like the other arts, builds on its past—an essential element of "fair use" under copyright law but one increasingly endangered by media corporations' efforts to control all copying. Ross tells us that rap music, with its incessant sampling, is the direct grandchild of avant-garde composition in the 1950s. Bob Dylan borrowed "The Times They Are A-Changing" from Bertolt Brecht and Hanns Eisler. Leonard Bernstein and Stephen Sondheim's *West Side Story* quotes Beethoven's Emperor Concerto (and of course borrows its plot from *Romeo and Juliet*).

Ross doesn't dwell on the tantalizing relation between music and politics, but he does offer one coda. "The aftermath of Hitler's corrosive love of music is unavoidable," he writes. "Much of subsequent twentieth-century musical history is a struggle to come to terms with it." Art and politics cannot be separated, he says, but

> it is equally false to claim the opposite, that art can somehow be swallowed up in history or irreparably damaged by it. Music may not be inviolable, but it is infinitely variable, acquiring a new identity in the mind of every new listener. It is always in the world, neither guilty nor innocent, subject to the ever-changing human landscape in which it moves (306-07).

December 22, 2007

For more on copyright and fair use, see Marjorie Heins and Tricia Beckles, *Will Fair Use Survive? Free Expression in the Age of Copyright Control* (Free Expression Policy Project/Brennan Center for Justice, 2005), http://ncac.org/fepp-articles/will-fair-use-survive-free-expression-in-the-age-of-copyright-control.

# Part Four:
Structural Challenges, Private Censorship Pressures, and the Delicate Balance Between Freedom of Religion and Separation of Church and State

# Structural Free Expression Issues: Copyright, Government Funding, and Media Democracy

An earlier version of this essay was given as a talk at the University of Buffalo Center for the Arts and UB Law School Baldy Center for Law & Social Policy, Workshop on Government Policy, Cultural Production, Personal Privacy, 9/10/2004.

Thank you for inviting me to participate in this fascinating, eclectic, cross-disciplinary exploration of "Government Policy, Cultural Production, and Personal Privacy." My contribution, "Structural Free Expression Issues," is, I admit, not the sexiest one in the annals of artistic freedom and censorship. A few years back, when I worked for the American Civil Liberties Union and then began the Free Expression Policy Project (FEPP), I spent a lot of time thinking and talking about the somewhat racier subjects of sex and violence in American culture. But, as FEPP's work has developed, I've discovered that the very structure of our mass media and our system of laws and benefit programs has implications for free expression at least as profound as the particular targets of censorship.

That is, who gets to speak the loudest and oftenest in America? In what forums? Whose voices are muted or barely heard? What information is suppressed, marginalized, or difficult to find? If, as the Supreme Court said more than fifty years ago, the First Amendment "rests on the assumption that the widest possible dissemination of information from diverse and antagonistic sources is essential to the welfare of the public,"[1] then the answers to these questions, in the long run, have more sweeping ramifications than whether a particular art exhibit is censored, whether the manufacturer of a particular violent video game is sued for allegedly inspiring a crime, or even whether the Federal Communications Commission fines a TV station half a million dollars for the Janet Jackson "wardrobe malfunction."[2]

Today, I want to address three structural free-expression issues: first, how our copyright system is designed and actually operates; second, who controls the mass media; and third, how information is manipulated through government funding and benefit programs.

## The Copyright System

Recent changes in law and technology have distorted the traditional balance between copyright owners' right to control the copying and distribution of their creations and vital free expression "safety valves" that limit copyright owners' control, such as fair use and the public domain. So, for example, the Copyright Clause of the Constitution (Article I, Section 8) authorizes Congress to grant copyrights for "limited times"; the first copyright law set the term at fourteen years. The point was to give authors and inventors enough incentive to create by allowing them control over the sale and distribution of their works for a short time; then to move these creations into the public domain, where they could be freely borrowed, copied, and built upon to produce still more products of human ingenuity and imagination.

Slowly but steadily, Congress has undermined this "limited time" provision of the Constitution until, with its 1976 copyright law, it stretched the term of control to the life of the author plus fifty years for individuals and seventy-five years for corporations. Congress added another twenty years to this already generous allotment in 1998 with its Sonny Bono Copyright Term Extension Act, sometimes called the "Mickey Mouse law" because of the Disney Company's heavy lobbying for its passage. The copyright on the immortal cartoon rodent would have expired in 2003 if not for that latest term extension.

What does this abandonment of any reasonable interpretation of the constitutional mandate of "limited" copyright terms mean for art, culture, scholarship, and free expression? Let me give one example, from the many *amicus curiae* briefs submitted to the Supreme Court when it considered (and rejected) a constitutional challenge to the Sonny Bono law.[3] The College Art Association, the National Humanities Alliance, and other groups whose members study visual art explained in their brief that scholars assembling texts and databases often cannot locate the owners of copyrights in educationally valuable letters, songs, photos, and other documents. Indeed, most authors have neither the time nor the financial resources to do this gritty work of tracking down copyright permissions—though publishers generally expect them to. Without written permissions, most publishers won't include the materials.

As a result, said the College Art Association, there are "gaping holes" in such documentary compilations as *The Video Encyclopedia of the Twentieth Century*, a resource popular with researchers and teachers, and "Who Built America?," an award-winning CD-ROM series for high school and college students containing primary sources from the 1930s. The compilers of "Who Built America?" had great difficulty finding copyright owners, and those they found sometimes wanted large fees even where the works in question had no commercial value. Thus, the editors were forced to omit the Depression Era demagogue Huey Long's campaign song, "Every Man a King," as well as many clips from popular films of the time. They substituted government documents or other works in the public domain, but the result was an unbalanced picture of the era.

The brief described an art historian who was refused permission to use a photo of Pablo Picasso and one of his daughters because the copyright owner disagreed with the historian's analysis of Picasso's work. A publisher that planned a new critical edition of *Cane*, by the Harlem Renaissance author Jean Toomer, in part to counterbalance the bias against Toomer reflected in the only available edition, could not go ahead because of the copyright term extension on *Cane*. "In the past," the brief said, "researchers could anticipate and plan on new material becoming available for unrestricted use on a constant and continuing basis." But the law's 20-year "moratorium on the public domain" upsets those expectations and penalizes scholars, museums, teachers, and historians. All this in the interest of further enriching a relatively few copyright owners "who already have received significant value from their ownership under the preexisting term."[4]

Thus, it is not only the generalized effects on art and culture that are of concern when the public domain is frozen due to Congress' continuing extensions of the "limited time" of copyright. It is also the ability of copyright owners to censor ideas they don't like, as illustrated by the examples of Jean Toomer's *Cane* and Picasso's family photographs.

Congress created another structural problem in 1998 with the Digital Millennium Copyright Act, which essentially gives the force of law to "digital rights management" technologies, developed by media corporations to prevent unauthorized access to copyrighted works. The DMCA makes it a crime to circumvent such technologies, even for purposes of fair use under copyright law. Fair use is an important free expression safety valve that allows limited copying for such purposes as scholarship, journalism, commentary, and parody.

So, for example, a scholar who wants to copy a few frames of a film classic to show her class—a legitimate fair use—violates the DMCA if she circumvents encryption in order to access and copy even a small part of the film. Courts have recognized that the DMCA cripples the exercise of fair use, but so far have upheld the law anyway, as a justified congressional response to industry fears of illegal copying and lost income.[5]

It's difficult to measure the cultural impact of these changes in the structure of the copyright system, but just as the increasing consolidation of the publishing industry in ever-fewer hands, and its drive for ever-larger profit margins dramatically affects what books are promoted and distributed, so the difficulties of our film scholar and millions like her in exercising their fair use rights have wide-ranging systemic effects.

## The Structure of Mass Communications

Mass media consolidation is my second structural free expression issue. The Federal Communications Commission's decision last year to relax its rules limiting the percent of national audience that any single media company can reach, and restricting various forms of media cross-ownership and multiple ownership in local markets, gave rise to widespread protests; this June, a federal court overturned nearly all of the FCC's order.[6] These battles over further media consolidation of an already dangerously concentrated industry, in which six corporate conglomerates control nearly eighty percent of network television content and one company, Clear Channel, owns more than 1,200 radio stations,[7] are important, but there is a more basic problem with our current mass media structure.

The problem starts with a system of broadcast regulation that first proclaims the airwaves to be a national resource, communally owned, that should be dedicated to serving the public interest; then turns over virtually all of the broadcast spectrum to commercial entities that are essentially in the business—to use the straightforward terminology of the industry—of delivering eyeballs to advertisers. Radio and TV companies that enjoy the scarce privilege of a broadcast license are supposed to serve the public interest: to provide art, entertainment, and news from a range of viewpoints, to cover issues and events of local interest, and to reflect the cultural diversity of our population. But these lofty principles inevitably conflict with both the profit-maximizing goal of media corporations and the political interests of their owners, and attempts to enforce them have been both intermittent and ineffective.

A mandated few hours per week of so-called educational programming, for example, and a statutory requirement that broadcasters give equal time to candidates for office, do not go very far when the TV broadcaster still chooses the program content, reduces the amount of time spent on political reportage (as opposed to airing lucrative but often deceptive campaign ads), and suppresses anything that its owners deem politically inconvenient. Michael Moore had the wherewithal to find other means of reaching the American public when the Walt Disney Company refused to distribute his movie *Fahrenheit 9/11* because the company did not want to offend Florida Governor Jeb Bush,[8] but most media corporations' forays into political self-censorship do succeed in suppressing or marginalizing controversial speech. The examples are legion: from Sinclair Broadcasting, which owns 62 TV stations, refusing to air a Nightline program focusing on American military deaths in Iraq, to Time Warner-owned CNN's rejecting an ad from the Log Cabin Republicans urging tolerance on gay issues.[9]

The solution must start where the problem began: not with "deregulation," as free-market theorists suggest, but with the restructuring of a broadcast system that turns over the public airwaves almost entirely to for-profit corporations.

Another current battle over media regulation involves cable broadband Internet access. The issue here is whether this increasingly popular means of getting online will be treated as a "telecommunications service" like the phone company, and therefore a common carrier which cannot control the content of speech that goes over its wires, or as an unregulated "information service," which can exercise content control, discriminate against Web sites it dislikes, and refuse to allow other service providers to sell Internet access over its cables. The FCC supports the cable industry's claim to be an "information service" for purposes of broadband access; the Ninth Circuit Court of Appeals recently overturned that FCC ruling, and both the government and the cable industry are asking for Supreme Court review.[10] It does not take a rocket scientist to see that if the FCC wins this case, monopolistic cable companies could quickly transform the Internet from a worldwide soapbox with easy access to vast and diverse resources, into mass medium dominated by games, shopping, and homogeneous, often superficial news and entertainment. (Social media, dominated by megaliths like Facebook and Twitter, admittedly have a more participatory business model, but it's still the owners who ultimately decide who gets to say what.)

## The Structure of Government Funding

My third example of a structural free expression issue involves conditions on government benefits or funding. Because the First Amendment limits government's ability to control speech directly, it often uses the carrot-and-stick approach of funding private speech. That is—to take one well-known example—Congress passes a law prohibiting funding for art that is thought to violate "general standards of decency" or lack "respect" for the "diverse beliefs and values of the American public." In 1998, the Supreme Court upheld this law restricting the National Endowment for the Arts' discretion in awarding grants. The Court reasoned that although the First Amendment would not allow Congress to impose these sorts of vague ideological restrictions directly, they are perfectly reasonable criteria for federal spending.[11]

This was, perhaps, a prudent decision, given the highly charged politics of arts funding. And it is true, as opponents of free expression in arts funding never tire of pointing out, that artists are free to create whatever they want "on their own time, and their own dime." But there is no denying that "decency" and "respect" criteria for federal arts grants have a widespread systemic effect on the visibility of controversial art within our culture indeed, on the very financial ability to create it. Government grants leverage significant amounts of private money, not to mention prestige.

And although to many, the Supreme Court's decision seemed reasonable in the context of arts funding, just try applying it to a government-funded institution such as a university. A law prohibiting all faculty and staff from engaging in any expression that violates "general standards of decency and respect for the diverse beliefs and values of the American public" would have profoundly negative effects on classroom discussion, extracurricular activities, and the research and writing of professors, not to mention on-campus political debate.

Another funding law, mandating Internet filters on all computers in libraries that receive federal aid for Internet connections, or even just the benefit of a federally mandated e-rate discount, was also upheld by the Supreme Court last year—reversing a lower court decision that detailed the irrationality of filters' operations, and the tens of thousands of valuable Web sites they block, even at their narrowest settings.[12]

This was Congress' third attempt to restrict expression online, and the irony is that the Supreme Court struck down the first two laws even though they would have had much less sweeping censorship effects than the third law, mandating Internet filters. The reason for the difference: the first two laws directly banned speech deemed "indecent" or "harmful to minors"[13]; the third technically did not ban anything—it simply gave libraries a choice: if you think Internet filters are dangerous tools that contradict the very core of a library's mission, the answer is simple: don't accept e-rate discounts or government funds.

Of course, it is an illusory choice for many libraries, especially the ones in lower income communities for which the e-rate was created. Building censorship into the structure of funding and other benefit programs enables government to establish a systemic regime of disfavoring and disadvantaging non-mainstream and provocative art and ideas more pervasively than it could ever do by means of direct censorship.

The same sort of structural free expression problems exist, as I've suggested, under the systems in place to govern copyright and the mass media industry. The challenge today is to understand how these structures impact free expression, and find ways to promote systemic change.

## Notes

1. *Associated Press v. United States*, 326 U.S. 1, 20 (1945).

2. See "What is the Fuss About Janet Jackson's Breast?" in this volume.

3. *Eldred v. Ashcroft*, 537 U.S. 186 (2003).

4. Brief of the College Art Association, *et al.* as *Amici Curiae* in Support of Petitioners, *Eldred v. Ashcroft* (5/20/2002), 13, 7-10, as described in Free Expression Policy Project, *The Progress of Science and Useful Arts: Why Copyright Today Threatens Intellectual Freedom* (2003), 16, http://ncac. org/wp-content/uploads/2017/10/marjie6.pdf. The other signers of this brief were the Visual Resources Association, National Humanities Alliance, Consortium of College and University Media Centers, and National Initiative for a Networked Cultural Heritage.

5. *Universal City Studios v. Corley*, 273 F.3d 429, 459 (2nd Cir. 2001); *United States v. Elcom Ltd.*, 203 F. Supp.2d 1125, 1131 (N.D. Cal. 2002).

6. *Prometheus Radio Project v. FCC*, 373 F.3d 37 (3rd Cir. 2004).

7. Free Press, "Media Ownership Rules," http://www. freepress.net/rules/page.php?n=fcc (accessed 2004); and www.freepress.net generally; Leonard Hill, "The Hijacking of Hollywood," in *News Incorporated* (Elliot Cohen, ed., 2005), 220.

8. Jim Rutenberg, "Disney is Blocking Distribution of Film That Criticizes Bush," *NY Times*, 5/5/2004, http://www.nytimes.com/2004/05/05/us/disney-is-blocking-distribution-of-film-that-criticizes-bush.html.

9. Bill Moyers, "The Media, Politics, and Censorship," 5/10/2004, http://www.commondreams.org/views04/0510-10.htm (Sinclair); Mark Memmott, "Gay GOP Group Criticizes CNN's Rejection of Ad," *USA Today*, 8/31/2004.

10. *Brand X Internet Services v. FCC*, 345 F.3d 1120 (9th Cir. 2003), reversed, *National Cable & Telecommunications Assn v. Brand X Internet Services*, 545 U.S. 967 (2005) (upholding the FCC's position that broadband carriers are not "telecommunications services").

11. *National Endowment for the Arts v. Finley*, 524 U.S. 569 (1998).

12. *United States v. American Library Association*, 539 U.S. 194 (2003).

13. *Ashcroft v. American Civil Liberties Union*, 542 U.S. 656

(2004) (affirming a preliminary ruling that a criminal law banning "harmful to minors" speech online is probably unconstitutional); *Reno v. American Civil Liberties Union*, 521 U.S. 844 (1997) (striking down a criminal law banning "indecent" speech online). See "'Our Children's Hearts, Minds—and Libidos': What's at Stake in the COPA Case," in this volume.

# Disney, Media Giants, and Corporate Control

Here is a First Amendment quiz. Which is the biggest threat to free expression in America today:

(1) The Walt Disney Company's announcement two weeks ago that it will not permit its Miramax subsidiary to distribute Michael Moore's film *Fahrenheit 9/11*.[1]

(2) Disney's alleged reason for the ban: fear that Florida Governor Jeb Bush will punish Disney if it distributes the film, by undermining lucrative tax deals for Disney theme parks.

(3) Ownership of ever-larger chunks of our culture by media conglomerates such as Disney.

If you guessed number 3, you are right.

Michael Moore will find another distributor for *Fahrenheit 9/11*. In fact, last week Disney announced that it would sell the rights to Miramax founders Bob and Harvey Weinstein, so that they can arrange for another distributor. And Moore's expert orchestration of the news of Disney's decision, as well as his own well-deserved reputation as a trenchant critic of U.S. policy and culture, almost guarantee that a distributor will be found.

Disney's alleged reason for its decision is more troubling than the decision itself. The likelihood that a political official (here, Jeb Bush) would retaliate against a taxpayer (here, Disney) for communicating information and ideas distasteful to the official is, perhaps, just a cynical recognition of political realities. But it would be unconstitutional for Governor Bush to manipulate his state's tax policies in this fashion, and for good reason.

Protecting speech critical of the government is a core function of the First Amendment. If political officials can punish such criticism by withdrawing tax breaks or other benefits, then the result will be to suppress expression that is the basis of democracy. For this reason, courts have consistently ruled that it is unconstitutional for government officials to wield their power to retaliate against unwelcome speech.

By contrast, censorship by private corporations generally doesn't create First Amendment problems. Disney and other mega-corporations have the right to decide which of the projects owned or generated by their many affiliates and subsidies they want to publish, broadcast, or distribute, and which (such as *Fahrenheit 9/11*) they want to quash. Technically, there is no First Amendment violation when Disney censors Michael Moore, or—to take another of numerous recent examples—when Viacom, whose CEO supported George W. Bush for president, refused to air independent political advertisements, including a critical ad by MoveOn.org during the Super Bowl broadcast.[2]

Why, then, is the formidable size and economic power of media corporations arguably the gravest threat to free expression in the U.S. today? Because as these companies grow ever bigger, the ability to decide what news, information, and political commentary most Americans will hear becomes concentrated in fewer hands. The formerly independent Miramax is now controlled by Disney. Independent book publishers have been swallowed up by corporate conglomerates like Bertelsmann and Viacom.[3]

Most critically for democracy, the public depends on the media to uncover political malfeasance—including, most recently, the criminal conduct of the American military at Abu Ghraib prison in Baghdad. If this essential function is concentrated in the hands of a few media powerhouses that are too cozy with those in power, we lose access to the information that we need to govern ourselves.

As the Supreme Court explained more than fifty years ago, a democracy cannot function well without "the widest possible dissemination of information from diverse and antagonistic sources."[4] Whether the issue is Disney's censorship of Moore in order to curry favor with President Bush's brother or Viacom's suppression of MoveOn.org for similar reasons, these events are only worrisome if Disney and Viacom are powerful enough to control the information and ideas that reach most Americans.

The Federal Communications Commission has a mandate to control media consolidation, but in the past few years, it has woefully failed to do so. Meanwhile, the agency wastes its time and the taxpayers' money on political sideshows, such as its recent "indecency" rulings against the televised effusions of rock star Bono and the flatulence jokes of radio "shock jock" Howard Stern.

*Fahrenheit 9/11*, of course, is a reference to *Fahrenheit 451*, Ray Bradbury's 1953 novel about censorship, and the 1966 François Truffaut film of the same name. The title denotes the temperature at which book paper catches fire.

May 21, 2004

## Notes

1. Jim Rutenberg, "Disney is Blocking Distribution of Film That Criticizes Bush," *NY Times*, 5/5/2004, http://www.nytimes.com/2004/05/05/us/disney-is-blocking-distribution-of-film-that-criticizes-bush.html.

2. Fairness and Accuracy in Media, "Viacom Blocking Independent Political Ads," 10/18/2004, https://fair.org/take-action/action-alerts/viacom-blocking-independent-political-ads; Leonard Hill, "The Hijacking of Hollywood," in *News Incorporated* (Elliot Cohen, ed., 2005), 224.

3. Free Press, "Media Ownership Rules," http://www.freepress.net/rules/page.php?n=fcc (accessed 2004); and www.freepress.net generally.

4. *Associated Press v. United States*, 326 U.S. 1, 20 (1945).

# The Attack on Science

Sometimes private corporations, their voices amplified by generous spending on the election campaigns of our political leaders, have an inordinate effect not only on government policy but on the supposedly nonpartisan, disinterested dissemination of scientific information. Sometimes religious pressure groups have a similarly powerful distorting effect on scientific truth. From environmental hazards to sex education, the federal government in the past several years has been responding to these pressures by twisting science to political ends. The ends are sometimes ideological—as in the suppression of information about condoms and sexual safety—and sometimes simply take the form of favors to business interests that would like to see less environmental, public health, or workplace safety regulation. But the pattern has become so pervasive that much of the scientific community is up in arms.

## The Beginnings

Concern about the George W. Bush administration's manipulation and distortion of science goes back at least to July 2003, when the Interior Department introduced a new book into the Grand Canyon National Park's official bookstore. Titled *Grand Canyon: A Different View*, the book takes issue with extensive geological evidence that the canyon evolved over several million years, and instead argues that the canyon was forged by a single "catastrophic" event only a few thousand years ago: the great flood of biblical fame.

Leading geological associations protested this introduction of Creationism into the National Park Service's educational programs. They pointed out that a major purpose of the

Park Service is "to promote the use of sound science in all its programs." The government's top geologist, David Shaver, explained that *A Different View* "purports to be science when it is not," and makes "claims that are counter to widely accepted geological evidence." Nevertheless, the book was reordered after stock ran out, and as of October 2004 was still being marketed by the Parks Service.[1]

If this conflict between science and religious fundamentalism was simply one more instance of biblical literalists' unending effort to undermine evolution, a report released just a month after the appearance of *A Different View* on government bookstore shelves detailed more contemporary distortions of science. Prepared by the Democratic staff of the House Government Reform Committee at the request of Congressman Henry Waxman, this report described the purging of safer-sex information from the Centers for Disease Control Web site, the posting of misinformation on the National Cancer Institute site that asserted an increased risk of breast cancer among women who have had abortions, and the suppression of information about lead poisoning, global warming, and prescription drug advertising, and about water pollution caused by the oil and gas industries.[2]

In February 2004, the Union of Concerned Scientists (UCS) released a similar, but longer and more detailed report. Divided into two parts, it first documented "Suppression and Distortion of Research Findings at Federal Agencies," including information on climate change (global warming), air quality (mercury emissions from power plants and other air pollutants), reproductive health (sex education, HIV-AIDS, and the alleged breast cancer-abortion link), airborne bacteria, Iraq's aluminum tubes (erroneously claimed by the administration to be part of a nuclear weapons program), endangered species, and forest management. The second part of the UCS report, "Undermining the Quality and Integrity of the Appointment Process," described the purging of qualified scientists from federal advisory panels, the appointment of less qualified, and often industry-connected replacements, and the vetting of panel candidates with political questions such as whether they had voted for President Bush and would support his policies.[3]

These political litmus tests for scientific advisory panels were particularly troubling, for they evidenced a basic misunderstanding of the panels' purposes. Scientific advisory committees are supposed to provide objective, unbiased information to guide government officials in making policy that will protect public health, occupational safety, and the environment—not to give an extra boost to the desires of for-profit corporations or an aura of respectability to policies that business and political leaders have decided upon in advance.

## Ideological Appointments

Perhaps the starkest example of ideology trumping science in the appointment of advisors was the selection of Dr. W. David Hager to the Food and Drug Administration's Reproductive Health Advisory Committee. The UCS report recounted that the administration initially suggested Hager as chair of the FDA committee, but "after widespread public outcry" because of his "scant credentials and highly partisan political views," the administration settled for making him a committee member rather than the chair. The report noted that Hager "is best known for co-authoring a book that recommends particular scripture readings as a treatment for premenstrual syndrome and, in his private practice, Hager has reportedly refused to prescribe contraceptives to unmarried women."[4]

Accompanying the UCS's February 2004 report was a strongly worded statement of concern by 62 leading scientists, including 20 Nobel Prize winners. "Successful application of science has played a large part in the policies that have made the United States of America the world's most powerful nation and its citizens increasingly prosperous and healthy," the statement began. "Although scientific input to the government is rarely the only factor in public policy decisions, this input should always be weighed from an objective and impartial perspective to avoid perilous consequences." But the Bush administration had disregarded this principle by "placing people who are professionally unqualified or who have clear conflicts of interest in official posts and on scientific advisory committees," and by censoring reports by "the government's own scientists. ... Other administrations have, on occasion, engaged in such practices, but not so systematically nor on so wide a front."[5]

The administration quickly responded. The director of the President's Office of Science and Technology Policy, John Marburger III, issued a statement the same day as the scientists', accusing them of making "sweeping generalizations ... based on what appears to be a miscellany of criticisms" largely from "partisan political figures and advocacy organizations."[6]

Marburger followed up in April 2004 with a twenty-page single-spaced rebuttal to the UCS report. It touted Bush Administration expenditures and achievements, insisted that advisory committee appointees are put through a "rigorous selection process," and otherwise emphasized the positive—for example, that CIA Director George Tenet had acknowledged that none of Iraq's aluminum tubes found so far met the specifications for nuclear weapons; that the President had appointed Democrats to science advisory panels; and that the misleading statements about abortion and breast cancer had been revised after further review. Marburger also acknowledged that an Environmental Protection Agency report on mercury emissions should not have copied directly from an industry memo.[7]

But as the UCS painstakingly pointed out in its reply to Marburger two weeks later, "aside from a couple of minutiae, the White House document fails to offer much evidence to support its claims," and instead "offers irrelevant information and fails to address the central point of many charges in the UCS report." Reviewing the record on mercury emissions, climate change, abstinence-only education, HIV/AIDS, breast cancer, airborne bacteria, Iraq's aluminum tubes, endangered species, lead poisoning, forest management, workplace safety, and political litmus tests for advisory panels, the UCS pointed out that Marburger had not in fact denied many of the charges.[8]

## The Attack on Enlightenment Values

The next salvo was fired by the UCS in July 2004, when it published a follow-up report. It documented administration actions that:

- minimized findings on the environmental devastation caused by strip mining;

- prevented approval of over-the-counter sale of an emergency contraceptive despite advisory panel consensus on its safety (the drug is available without prescription in 33 other countries);

- used flawed science in Fish and Wildlife Service findings on endangered species (Florida panthers, bull trout, and rare swans); and

- continued to pose partisan political questions to advisory committees nominees (*e.g.,* "what I thought about President Bush: did I like him, what did I think of the job he was doing…"[9]).

The introduction to this second report quoted UCS board chair and physicist Kurt Gottfried: "The absence of a candid and constructive response from the White House is troubling, as these issues—from childhood lead poisoning and mercury emissions to climate change and nuclear weapons—have serious consequences for public health, well-being, and national security."[10]

The UCS's concerns were well publicized, and led to a lengthy *New York Times* article in October 2004. It quoted Marburger explaining that "this administration really does not like regulation and it believes in market processes …, so there's always going to be a tilt in an administration like this one to a certain set of actions that you take to achieve some policy objective." The *Times* also quoted one marine ecologist who had been nominated for the Arctic Research Commission and was asked as the first interview question from a White House staffer: "Do you support the president?" She replied that "she was not a fan of Mr. Bush's economic and foreign policies. … 'That was the end of the interview,' she said. 'I was removed from consideration instantly.'"[11]

By December 2004, more than 5,000 scientists had signed on to the original February 2004 statement of concern. Forty-eight are Nobel laureates, 62 are National Medal of

Science recipients, and 135 are members of the National Academy of Sciences. But despite the growing alarums, occasional embarrassing publicity, and continuing pressure from Congressman Waxman's office, there have been only sporadic retreats from the administration's politicization of science.

For example, a number of advisory panel nominations that were at first rejected, were later accepted after protest and pressure from leaders in the field. The misinformation about breast cancer and abortion was removed from the National Cancer Institute site and after several months, accurate information was restored. Most important, perhaps, the administration continues to claim its respect for science and deny that its policies are driven by business interests or the magical thinking of its fundamentalist base. As long as the administration accepts that scientific impartiality and integrity are the agreed-upon goals, there is the potential that publicity and pressure can prevent or reverse at least some partisan distortions of scientific findings.

The UCS has ambitious plans in this respect: further dissemination of information; organizing roundtables and support groups at universities across the country; toolkits of event planning materials; classroom resources; more publicity; working groups on the various scientific policy issues; and coordination with Rep. Waxman, who introduced legislation in late 2004 that would have created "an independent commission to investigate the politicization of science under the Bush administration." The legislation was defeated in a nearly party-line vote.[12]

In part, this battle over scientific integrity in government and in particular, the ways in which private industry has distorted the process, is part of a longer-term struggle for Enlightenment values and against theocratic yearnings in America. As Gary Wills recently wrote, "America, the first real democracy in history, was a product of Enlightenment values—critical intelligence, tolerance, respect for evidence, a regard for the secular sciences." But "can a people that believes more fervently in the Virgin Birth than in evolution [according to recent surveys] still be called an Enlightened nation?"[13]

The jury is still out.

December 7, 2004

**Update:** In late December, Rep. Waxman released another report, "The Content of Federally Funded Abstinence-Only Education Programs." It documented how American tax dollars are being spent in ever-larger amounts on programs that discourage students from using condoms by misrepresenting their failure rates, that contain false information about the risks of abortion, that blur science and religion, that perpetuate sex stereotypes (*e.g.,* women need "financial support," while men need "admiration"), and that contain numerous other scientific errors.

The report found that more than eighty percent of the abstinence-only curricula, used by more than two-thirds of the 2003 grantees in the largest federally funded program, called "SPRANS," "contain false, misleading, or distorted information about reproductive health." It concluded: "Serious and pervasive problems with the accuracy of abstinence-only curricula may help explain why these programs have not been shown to protect adolescents from sexually transmitted diseases and why youth who pledge abstinence are significantly less likely to make informed choices about precautions when they do have sex."[14]

## Notes

[I have updated some Web addresses since they were first accessed in December 2004. Others, which were active when accessed in December 2004, are no longer available.]

1. Esther Kaplan, *With God on Their Side: How Christian Fundamentalists Trampled Science, Policy, and Democracy in George W. Bush's White House* (2004), 91-94; Robert Longley, "Parks Service Sticks With Biblical Explanation for Grand Canyon," 10/19/2004, http://usgovinfo. about.com/od/rightsandfreedoms/a/canyonflood. htm.

2. Politics and Science in the Bush Administration, Report Prepared for Rep. Henry Waxman, U.S. House of Representatives, Committee on Government Reform (August 2003), http://democrats.reform.house.gov/ features/politics_and_science/report.htm.

3. Union of Concerned Scientists, Scientific Integrity in Policymaking: An Investigation Into the Bush Administration's Misuse of Science (Feb. 2004; updated March 2004), https://www.ucsusa.org/sites/default/ files/legacy/assets/documents/scientific_integrity/ rsi_final_fullreport_1.pdf.

4. *Id.*, 25.

5. Union of Concerned Scientists, 2004 Scientist Statement on Restoring Scientific Integrity to Federal Policy Making (2/18/2004), https://www.ucsusa.org/ our-work/center-science-and-democracy/promoting-

scientific-integrity/scientists-sign-on-statement.html#. WoSpNILrow.

6. Press Release, Office of Science and Technology Policy, Statement From President Bush's Science Advisor … on the Union of Concerned Scientists Document, 2/18/2004, http://ostp.gov/html/jhmStatementUCS report2-18-04.pdf.

7. Statement of the Honorable John H. Marburger, III On ScientificIntegrityintheBushAdministration(4/2/2004), http://ostp.gov/html/ucs/ResponsetoCongress onUCSDocumentApril2004.pdf.

8. Union of Concerned Scientists, Analysis of the April 2 Document from the White House Office of Science and Technology Policy on Scientific Integrity in the Bush Administration, 4/19/2004), http://www.ucsusa. org/global_environment/rsi/page.cfm?pageID=1393.

9. Union of Concerned Scientists, Scientific Integrity in Policy Making: Further Investigation of the Bush Administration's Misuse of Science, July 2004, 27, https://www.ucsusa.org/sites/default/files/legacy/ assets/documents/scientific_integrity/scientific_ integrity_in_policy_making_july_2004_1.pdf (quote from Dr. Richard Myers).

10. *Id.*, 5

11. Andrew Revkin, "Bush and the Laureates: How Science Became a Partisan Issue," *NY Times*, 10/19/2004, F1, F9.

12. "Reps. Waxman and Tierney Introduce Bill on Investigating the Politicization of Science," 5/17/2004, www.democrats.reform.house.gov/features/politics_

and_science/index.htm.

13. Gary Wills, "The Day the Enlightenment Went Out," *NY Times*, 11/4/2004, A25.

14. The Content of Federally Funded Abstinence-Only Education Programs, Report Prepared for Rep. Henry Waxman, U.S. House of Representatives, Committee on Government Reform - Minority Staff, Special Investigations Division (December 2004), i-ii, www. democrats.reform.house.gov. The SPRANS program, which funds many churches, had a budget of $75 million in fiscal year 2004; it will increase to $104 million in FY 2005. Other federal programs contribute a total of $63 million per year to distorted and inaccurate abstinence education.

# Trading Academic Freedom for Foreign Markets

The current controversy over Yale University's planned campus in Singapore is, at bottom, an argument over how much compromise on free speech is justified in exchange for the presumed benefits of locating branches of U.S. universities within authoritarian regimes. For although the champions of global ventures like Yale's often claim that academic freedom will be available at the foreign outposts, the fact is that such freedom, at best, will be limited to the classroom and will bear no resemblance to what we have come to expect on U.S. campuses. In Singapore, there is no freedom of speech; gay rights are nonexistent; and people are imprisoned for statements deemed critical of the regime.

In an April 2012 resolution, the Yale faculty expressed concern over the Singapore venture and urged administrators to respect and protect principles of nondiscrimination and civil liberties.[1] Yale's main defense was that this new campus is not really part of Yale but is a joint venture with the National University of Singapore ("NUS"); essentially, Yale has lent its name but Yale-NUS will not grant Yale degrees and will be paid for entirely by the host regime.[2]

Which, at least according to some, is precisely the problem. As one professor wrote, "despite the rhetoric, Yale-NUS is not a part of Yale. ... It will not teach Yale's curriculum, nor will Yale approve Yale-NUS courses. Its faculty will not be subject to Yale's rigorous appointment process."

Nevertheless, the publicity for the new college encourages one to believe that it is a part of Yale and that its degree will offer the same prestige as a real Yale degree. For example, the home page for Yale-NUS prominently displays a banner with the words "Yale-NUS College" against a Yale blue background, where "Yale" and "College" are in white, separated by the letters "NUS" in subdued orange.

He urged Yale (to no avail) to drop its name from the new venture.[3]

So Yale-NUS turns out to be primarily an exercise in commercial branding. But Yale is lending more than its name; Yale faculty will teach there; the Yale-NUS president, Pericles Lewis, is a former Yale professor, and the first dean, Charles D. Bailyn, currently teaches at Yale. Although Lewis told reporters that "we expect students to express all kinds of opinions on campus," he also acknowledged that off-campus, "students will have to abide by the laws of Singapore."[4]

Those laws include the strict censorship of films, broadcasting, print media, and the Internet, a Sedition Act, and a Public Order Act which requires a police permit to meet for any "cause related activity." As *The New York Times* noted, Singapore is "an autocratic city-state where drug offenses can bring the death penalty, homosexual relations are illegal and criminal defamation charges [against people who criticize public officials] are aggressively pursued."[5]

These laws will in fact limit Yale's promised freedom of speech on university grounds as well as off-campus. Lewis acknowledged to the *Wall Street Journal*: "The Singapore campus won't allow political protests, nor will it permit students to form partisan political societies."[6]

Much of the turmoil at Yale has to do with the concept of governance: the idea that at universities, the faculty should be active participants in the policy-making process. As Professor Christopher Miller told *Inside Higher Ed*: "When Yale went co-ed, the YCF [Yale College Faculty] voted. When, last year, there was a decision about bringing ROTC back, the YCF voted. But when there was a question about setting up the first sister campus bearing Yale's name in three hundred years, suddenly it was 'not a project of Yale College,' and we were not allowed to vote; the corporation acted on its own." Professor Seyla Benhabib, who introduced the faculty resolution, said that Singapore's "deplorable" record on human rights should have caused the administration to hesitate; moreover, "there are significant governance issues about faculty appointments, curriculum design and promotion procedures ... that have not been satisfactorily resolved."[7]

Before Yale came to global entrepreneurship, there was New York University blazing the trail, with a campus in Abu Dhabi, opened in 2010, and a planned campus in Shanghai, to open in September 2013. Unlike Yale, NYU will award its own degrees to the graduates. A March 2012 press release boasted that NYU Shanghai will be "the first American university with independent legal status approved by the [Chinese] Ministry of Education"; NYU president John Sexton exulted that "this is a magnificent day for NYU. ... New York and Shanghai enjoy a natural affinity as world capitals; as vibrant, ambitious, and forward-looking centers of commerce and culture; as magnets for people of talent."[8]

Like Yale, NYU announced that its new campus would respect academic freedom, but it soon became clear that at best, this applied only to classroom discussions; other on-campus activities would be subject to Chinese rules. "Academic freedom in China is curtailed by red lines around such sensitive subjects as political reform or Tibetan independence," the *Chronicle of Higher Education* reported in April; and quoted the new president of NYU Shanghai, Jeffrey Lehman: "Foreign students must realize they are not exempt from Chinese law."[9]

As a cautionary example, Bloomberg News published an article last year describing the 25-year-old Hopkins Nanjing Center, a joint project of Johns Hopkins and Nanjing Universities: in its entire existence, it has never published an academic journal, and when an American student, Brendon Stewart, tried in 2010, "he found out why. Intended to showcase the best work by Chinese and American students and faculty to a far-flung audience," the journal "broke the Hopkins-Nanjing Center's rules that confine academic freedom to the classroom. Administrators prevented the journal from circulating outside campus, and a student was pressured to withdraw an article about Chinese protest movements. About 75 copies sat in a box in Stewart's dorm room for a year. ... Most of the Chinese students involved in editing and layout asked Stewart to remove their names."[10]

The muzzling of the journal, according to the Bloomberg article, was just one example of "the compromises to academic freedom that some American universities make in China." On the eve of the twentieth anniversary of the Tiananmen Square protests that were brutally repressed in 1989, students discussed the events in an online Google group; one of them offered to screen a documentary about the protests in a student lounge. Chinese police monitoring the Internet conversation alerted the center's Chinese administrators, who contacted their American counterparts, who halted the film showing.

The Bloomberg article reported that "limits on academic

freedom are one reason" that Stanford and Columbia have not opened campuses in China, although Columbia has a study center in Beijing, and Stanford plans to open one on the campus of Peking University. Such centers host lectures and provide offices for visiting professors, but are easily exited, as Columbia President Lee Bollinger explained: "The one thing we have to do is maintain our academic integrity. ... There are too many examples of a strict and stern control that lead you to think that this is kind of an explosive mix.'" Stanford President John Hennessy said its center has no protection of academic freedom: "Even the ones you get are so scripted as to not be freedom as we imagine it in this country."[11]

Yet the rush to build more U.S.-style universities in authoritarian countries continues. "Many of our American institutions are being seduced by the promise of an infusion of much-needed wealth from China," Orville Schell of the Asia Society told the *Daily Beast*. In other words, China (like Singapore) pays the bills, and the new campuses are expected to be lucrative. The *Wall Street Journal*, referring to the Yale-Singapore project, put it in crasser marketing terms: "For Yale, the venture provides a chance to extend the university's brand to fast-growing Asian markets" (and, oh yes, "to help introduce the Western liberal-arts tradition to the region").[12]

Some administrators defend the tradeoff by attempting a semantic distinction between free speech and academic freedom. NYU's Sexton told *Bloomberg News* that although "students and faculty at the new [Shanghai] campus shouldn't assume they can criticize government leaders or policies without repercussions, ... I have no trouble distinguishing between rights of academic freedom and rights of political expression."[13] He did not explain why he thought academic freedom does not include criticism of government leaders or policies, whether in the classroom, elsewhere on campus, or outside its walls. And research, journal writing, campus protest, film showings, and "extramural speech" have long been aspects of academic freedom as understood in the U.S.

Is the tradeoff worth it? Apart from the economic incentives, creating these global "portals," as NYU calls them, is driven by a thirst for prestige: to be a world player. Is there an argument that building these bridges, even with the inevitable cost to academic freedom, might create pressure on repressive regimes for more open inquiry? Or is such an argument simply naïve? One of my Chinese students (for several years, I taught an undergraduate course on censorship in American law and culture at, yes, NYU) thinks that giving up nearly all freedom of speech is a reasonable tradeoff: "Most of the population (especially young people under fifty) acknowledge the abysmal state of censorship in China," she wrote to me. "However, no one is willing to stand up or speak out. I think it's important for Chinese students to experience freedom of expression (even in limited conditions), so they can solidify their beliefs and develop the courage and skills to change China for the better."

Professor Andrew Ross of NYU (in an essay for the *Chronicle of Higher Education*) wants to go beyond "the tiresome debate about balancing the virtuous contributions of our new branch campuses against the corrosive stain of operating in illiberal societies." But that doesn't mean accepting administrators' frankly financial motives. Foreign campuses "are social commitments," Ross writes, "entailing responsibilities that are not governed by the bottom line."[14]

For example, Ross recounts, when a lecturer at Paris-Sorbonne University Abu Dhabi was arrested for speaking out in favor of judicial and financial reforms, NYU President Sexton told concerned faculty "that they should learn how to be cultural relativists and respect the different norms of another country." That was "entirely the wrong response," Ross says, "and indicative of why we cannot afford to view foreign campuses purely as revenue-seeking ventures."

July 30, 2012

**Update:** The American Association of University Professors sent an open letter to the Yale University community in December 2012, asking sixteen questions about academic freedom, discrimination, and working conditions on its planned new campus in the repressive city-state of Singapore.[15] Yale did not respond to the questions.

An earlier version of this article is available at http://ncac. org/fepp-articles/trading-academic-freedom-for-foreign-markets, and on the Academe Blog, https://academeblog. org/2012/07/30/trading-academic-freedom-for-foreign-markets/.

## Notes

1. Gavan Gideon & Antonia Woodford, "Faculty Approve Yale-NUS Resolution," *Yale Daily News*, 4/6/2012, https://yaledailynews.com/blog/2012/04/06/faculty-approve-yale-nus-resolution/.

2. Tamar Lewin, "Faculty Gives Yale a Dose of Dissent Over Singapore," *NY Times*, 4/4/12, http://www.nytimes. com/2012/04/05/education/singapore-partnership-creates-dissension-at-yale.html?pagewanted=all.

3. Michael Fischer, "Yale-NUS is Not Yale," *Yale Daily News*, 3/23/2012, https://yaledailynews.com/blog/2012/03/23/fischer-yale-nus-is-not-yale/.

4. Sharon Chen, "Yale to Ensure Students in Singapore Have Freedom of Expression," *Bloomberg*, 7/6/2012, https://www.bloomberg.com/news/articles/2012-07-07/yale-to-ensure-students-in-singapore-have-freedom-of-expression.

5. Lewin, *supra*. This article also notes financial ties between Singapore and a number of Yale trustees.

6. Shibani Mahtani, "Singapore's Venture With Yale to Limit Protests," *Wall Street Journal*, 7/16/2012, https://www.wsj.com/articles/SB10001424052702303933704577530524046581142?KEYWORDS=yale+singapore.

7. Both quoted in Elizabeth Redden, "Whose Yale College?" *Inside Higher Ed*, 3/28/2012, https://academeblog.org/2012/07/30/trading-academic-freedom-for-foreign-markets/.

8. "NYU and Shanghai Partner to Create NYU-Shanghai," 3/27/2011, http://www.nyu.edu/about/news-publications/news/2011/march/nyu-and-shanghai-partner-to-create-nyu-shanghai.html.

9. Mary Hennock, "New Leader of NYU Shanghai Has Built Other Bridges to China," *Chronicle of Higher Education*, 4/29/2012, https://www.chronicle.com/article/New-Leader-of-NYU-Shanghai-Has/131730.

10. Oliver Staley & Daniel Golden, "China Halts U.S. Academic Freedom at Classroom Door for Colleges," Bloomberg, 11/28/2011, https://www.bloomberg.com/news/articles/2011-11-28/china-halts-u-s-college-freedom-at-class-door.

11. *Id.*

12. Isaac Stone Fish, "No Academic Freedom For China," *Daily Beast*, 11/22/2011, http://www.thedailybeast.com/no-academic-freedom-for-china.html; Mahtani, *supra.*

13. Staley & Golden, *supra.*

14. Andrew Ross, "Not Just Another Profit-Seeking Venture," *Chronicle of Higher Education*, 12/4/2011, https://www.chronicle.com/article/Not-Just Another/129935.

15. An Open Letter From the AAUP to the Yale Community, https://www.aaup.org/news/2012/open-letter-aaup-yale-community. (I was one of the authors.)

# The Crumbling Wall of Church-State Separation

The constitutional challenge to the phrase "under God" in the Pledge of Allegiance may be the highest-profile church/state case on the 2003-2004 Supreme Court calendar, but it is not the most important. When the Court hears argument on December 2, 2003 in the case of *Locke v. Davey*, the conflict it confronts will have not just symbolic but tangible real-world impact on the fabric of church/state separation.

The plaintiff in the case, Joshua Davey, is a student majoring in Pastoral Ministries at a religious college in Washington State. Davey qualified for a state-funded scholarship, but lost it when he declared his major. That was because Washington's constitution, like the constitutions of 36 other states, explicitly prohibits the expenditure of taxpayer funds for religious instruction. These common "anti-aid" provisions in state constitutions have multiple purposes: to avoid entanglements between churches and government agencies, to keep disagreements and competition among religious groups away from politics, and to respect the conscience of taxpayers who don't want to be forced to subsidize indoctrination in religious beliefs other than their own.

Once upon a time, it was thought that the U.S. Constitution—by way of the First Amendment's Establishment Clause ("Congress shall make no law respecting an establishment of religion ...")—also barred government funding for religious education. But a brilliantly successful legal and political strategy over the past two decades on the part of some organizations, litigants, and scholars has undone that once rarely challenged gospel. Today, the question whether government must fund clergy training if it funds other, secular education is up for grabs. Indeed, the case before the Supreme Court is Washington State's appeal from a federal appeals court decision that answered the question affirmatively. The appeals court ruled that Washington's ban on funding religious instruction amounts to "viewpoint discrimination," in violation of the First Amendment right to free exercise of religion.[1]

It is precisely this theory of viewpoint discrimination, combined with a superficially appealing but mistaken argument about the need for equal treatment of religious and secular education, that has provided the intellectual ammunition for the Court's reversal of direction on church/state issues. In the 1970s, if one thing seemed clear from the vaguely worded Establishment Clause, it was that tax money cannot be used to support religious practice, proselytizing, or instruction. The reasons were grounded in both the Establishment and Free Exercise Clauses of the First Amendment.

That is, the framers of the Constitution understood that forcing taxpayers to support religions different from their own would violate deeply felt scruples of conscience, would likely lead to religious warfare, and would inevitably entangle the government in the affairs of the dominant churches—the ones most likely to benefit from government largesse. Public funding thus undermines conscience both for congregations of the dominant churches and for adherents of minority religions—and atheists—who are forced to pay their bills.

Abiding by these principles, the Supreme Court ruled in the 1970s that government funds cannot be used for religious education; and, following those precedents, it said in 1985 that a school district cannot send public school teachers into parochial schools to provide remedial services. But in 1997, the Court overruled the remedial services decision and cast serious doubt on the earlier precedents.[2] Finally, in 2002, the justices upheld a state voucher program that, among other things, provided funds to help low income and minority children obtain private—overwhelmingly parochial—education and thereby escape the physical dangers and educational failures of inner city public schools.[3]

It did not hurt that the facts of this voucher case were so sympathetic. Two other recent challenges to state decisions not to fund religion also seemed compelling in their appeal to human sympathy. One involved a deaf student at a Catholic school who was denied a state-funded sign language interpreter; the other, a blind student who sought state-funded vocational rehabilitation services in order to pursue his ministry training. In both cases, the Supreme Court ruled that the Establishment Clause does not require the state to deny funding for the religious activity. The Court's reasoning relied on a distinction that only a lawyer could love: taxpayer funds would not go directly to the sectarian schools, but to individual students and parents whose private choices, rather than choices by the state, would produce only an "incidental" benefit to religion.[4]

But the Court did not rule in these cases that either the First Amendment's free exercise of religion clause, or the rule crafted to interpret its free speech clause to ban "viewpoint discrimination" by agencies of government, *requires* funding for religious education. Those are the questions in the case now before the Court—and are the inevitable next step in the political and legal campaign to undo church/state separation.

The whole point of the Establishment Clause—and, even more forcefully, of state constitutional "anti-aid" provisions—is to make religion an exception to neutral government funding programs. The Constitution treats religious activity differently from secular activity; religious speech differently from speech with secular viewpoints; religious education differently from secular education, because it is best for religious citizens, atheist citizens, and the peace and happiness of our pluralistic society, that government steer clear of financing sectarian enterprises.

The American Center for Law & Justice, representing the student Joshua Davey, argues that the state's "purposeful discrimination against religious exercise" violates both the free speech and free exercise of religion clauses of the First Amendment. If this is so, then a state's refusal to support the rebuilding of church altars if it funds the rehabilitation of other rundown buildings would also violate the Free Exercise Clause; and its failure to pay the salaries of nuns teaching at parochial schools would constitute unconstitutional discrimination if it has a program to supplement the salaries of teachers at secular private schools. Which may be exactly the direction we are heading if the current juggernaut to undo church/state separation continues.

October 29, 2003

**Update:** On February 24, 2004, the Supreme Court, in an opinion by Chief Justice William Rehnquist, upheld Washington's "anti-aid" provision. Although Washington can choose to fund religious education, Rehnquist wrote, it is not required to do so. He noted that many states choose to avoid religious conflict by prohibiting tax funds to support the ministry.[5]

An earlier version of this article was published on Alternet. org

## Notes

1. *Locke v. Davey*, 299 F.3d 748 (9th Cir. 2002), reversed, 540 U.S. 712 (2004).

2. *Agostini v. Felton*, 521 U.S. 203 (1997).

3. *Zelman v. Simmons-Harris*, 536 U.S. 639 (2002).

4. *Zobrest v. Catalina Foothills School District*, 509 U.S. 1 (1993); *Witters* v. *Washington Department of Services for the Blind*, 474 U.S. 481 (1986).

5. *Locke v. Davey*, 540 U.S. 712 (2004).

# On Human Frailty and Public Interest Law

## Review of *Worst Instincts: Cowardice, Conformity, and the ACLU,* by Wendy Kaminer (2009)

In 2004, The *New York Times* published the first in a series of articles detailing bitter feuds within the American Civil Liberties Union (the ACLU), the country's premier civil liberties organization. The headlines tell the story:

12/18/04: "ACLU's Search for Data on Donors Stirs Privacy Fears"

1/21/05: "ACLU Will Consider Disciplining Two Officials"

6/5/05: "Concerns Arise at ACLU Over Document Shredding"

5/24/06: "ACLU May Block Criticism by Its Board"

6/18/06: "ACLU Board Members Debate Limits on Their Own Speech"

6/19/06: "ACLU Warned on Plan to Limit Members' Speech"

7/12/06: "ACLU Withdraws Proposals to Limit Public Criticism by Board"

9/26/06: "Supporters of ACLU Call for the Ouster of its Leaders"

These articles reported that a handful of ACLU national board members had been raising pointed questions about the actions of the organization's new executive director, Anthony Romero. Among the accusations:

- That the ACLU was data-mining information about its contributors, in violation of the group's principles and possibly of New York law governing charitable organizations.

- That Romero failed to report to the board on a settlement with the state attorney general on the data-mining issue within the time required by the settlement agreement.

- That the ACLU agreed to check its employees against the government's notoriously inaccurate terrorism watch lists, as a condition of remaining in a program allowing federal workers to make salary deductions to charitable organizations.

- That Romero falsely told the board that lawyers had advised him that he didn't really have to check the watch lists.

Depending upon one's point of view, these were either major departures from the ACLU's core principles or minor errors that any new executive might make, and that were more than outweighed by Romero's considerable talents, particularly in fundraising. But the conflict went deeper: some viewed the dissident board members' conversations with reporters from the *Times* and elsewhere as deplorable violations of fiduciary responsibility. The writer Wendy Kaminer, who was at the center of this storm and a board member at the time, clearly thought the opposite—that her fiduciary responsibility, not to mention her principles, forced her to go public after most of the board had circled the wagons in defense of Romero.

Although a number of Kaminer's fellow board members agreed with her and her major ally on the board, Michael Meyers, that the leadership's irregularities and departures from civil liberties principle were serious, they ultimately lost their battle to unseat Romero. Kaminer has now written a book documenting and reflecting on what happened.

It is far from a grudge book or a simple insider tale of hypocrisy in the high echelons of public interest advocacy and law. Although *Worst Instincts* reflects the author's understandable desire to set out a clear record of what happened and what was at stake, Kaminer is also a canny and thoughtful observer of human and institutional behavior. Her opening chapter insightfully reflects on the herd instinct and the pressures for conformity that sometimes prevent even dedicated individuals like those who comprise the ACLU's national board from standing up for principle when faced with the risk of ostracism from the group.

What the book lacks is a balanced reflection on the frailties of human nature and the inevitable deviations from moral purity that befall even the most high-minded organizations. Kaminer seems to acknowledge that she is uncompromising in her expectations. (She jokes at one point that although she can be difficult, her colleague Mike Meyers "makes me look like Mary Tyler Moore.") Her narrative casts Romero and his supporters in a dismal light, but she is mistaken to assume that his predecessor, Ira Glasser, reigned at the ACLU for twenty-three years without also encountering questions about his management style.

Perhaps it is in the nature of executive directors to attract "yes men" and women who will confound loyalty to the boss with loyalty to the organization, and will sometimes put both above loyalty to core principles. It was during the Glasser era that the ACLU became significantly more centralized: as the national office acquired more control over contributions, the state affiliates felt the loss of independence, and some bridled against it. Centralization, and the difficult balance between the priorities of funders and the demands of civil liberties, did not begin with Romero—and I am sure they are not unique to the ACLU. (I was an attorney in the ACLU national office from 1991-98, and before that, at the Massachusetts affiliate.)

During Glasser's watch, the ACLU's premier project, on reproductive freedom, staged a dramatic surprise departure from the organization because of dissatisfaction with programmatic and financial policies. Although some board members questioned Glasser about this, he deftly diverted any serious inquiry into underlying internal problems. The ACLU under Glasser was not the paragon of openness and lively board oversight that Kaminer imagines.

Kaminer raises profound and difficult questions about organizational integrity, politics, and personal loyalty. Peer pressures, herd mentality, and deviation from principle exist everywhere, but they are certainly more striking in nonprofit organizations that are dedicated to advancing justice, fairness, and openness. Were the compromises with civil liberties principles and basic honesty as dire as Kaminer and Meyers thought? On balance, was it worthwhile to "go public," at whatever cost to the organization's image or fundraising? Were they right to conclude that the ACLU had been so hopelessly corrupted that only an open airing of their concerns would save it?

Whatever the answer to these questions, the reaction of some ACLU people to Kaminer's and Meyer's muckraking was, in her telling, gratuitously insulting, and at least one institutional response contributed mightily to the public embarrassment. A proposal to limit board members' communications with the media, as detailed by *The New York Times* in the spring of 2006 (see the headlines quoted above) was one of the politically dumber proposals to be considered by a group whose primary cause is freedom of speech.

Putting aside that gaffe, what can one conclude from Kaminer's chronicle? Yes, there is human weakness, arrogance, and clannishness in all organizations, perhaps particularly at the top. At the ACLU, though, it is the affiliates, grounded in their local communities, that do the vital, sometimes astounding day-to-day work that is the heart and soul of the organization's mission.

It was the Massachusetts affiliate in 1968 that saw the civil liberties issues in the government's prosecution of Dr. Benjamin Spock and four other prominent activists for advocating disobedience to the Selective Service law as a form of resistance to the war in Vietnam, when the national organization wanted to steer clear of the case. It was California ACLUers who insisted on representing Fred Korematsu in his challenge to the government's internment of Japanese-Americans during World War II; the national office didn't want to get involved. It was the national ACLU board that caved in to anti-communist witch hunting when it ousted one of its founders, Elizabeth Gurley Flynn, for her Communist Party membership—i.e., for her expression and beliefs.

Yet the ACLU is a great institution, and American freedoms would be in a significantly more perilous state without it. Which doesn't mean that it can't do better. One can only hope that the ACLU's members and leaders will take Kaminer's book to heart instead of dismissing it—and her—with *ad hominem* attacks, as they sometimes did during the course of the battles she recounts.

May 1, 2009

# Part Five:
## Intellectual Property and Fair Use

# You Can Play Fantasy Baseball Without a License, But Can You Google It?

Two controversies in the past week highlighted the lengths to which some folks will go in trying to control language and information. The first involved that venerable American sit-down sport, fantasy baseball; the second concerned a newer, but even more popular pastime, "googling" on the Internet.

## No Monopoly on Baseball Stats

On August 8, 2006, U.S. Magistrate Judge Mary Ann Medler ruled that the Major League Baseball Players Association and its interactive media arm, called Major League Baseball Advanced Media, can't stop fantasy game Web sites from using baseball players' names, batting averages, and other statistics. The Players Association has long insisted that it has the right to license (or not) fantasy baseball games.

The C.B.C. Distribution Company, maker of fourteen such games, had filed suit asking for a declaratory judgment that it does not need a license. Magistrate Medler agreed, writing in her decision that both the players' names and their statistics are in the "public domain"—readily available in newspapers and other media.[1]

The decision turned on the "right of publicity" recognized in the laws of 28 states. Advanced Media had initially claimed that fantasy baseball also violated federal copyright and trademark law, but later agreed to dismiss those claims, probably because it recognized that statistical information is not covered by copyright, and the simple use of players' names in these circumstances was not a trademark violation.

(It would have been a stronger trademark case if C.B.C. used players' pictures or team logos.)

The right of publicity gives celebrities control over the use of their identities for commercial purposes such as advertising. For example, it prevents companies from using a celebrity's name or photo to sell a product without the celebrity's consent (which usually involves a large infusion of dollars for the endorsement). One famous case involved the "Here's Johnny" Portable Toilet company—a clever pun, but one that TV personality Johnny Carson did not appreciate. ("Here's Johnny" was the famous tag line on Carson's late-night show.) The court held in that case that the potty company had unlawfully exploited Carson's identity to obtain a commercial advantage.[2]

The right of publicity, obviously, doesn't prevent biographers from writing about celebrities or journalists from covering news events. In a 1977 case, though, the Supreme Court recognized the right of publicity of a performer called "the human cannonball" when a TV station broadcast his performance without his permission. The Court rejected that station's argument that it had a First Amendment right to televise the show which trumped the state-law right of publicity.[3]

In the fantasy baseball case, Magistrate Medler ruled against the right of publicity because "there is nothing about CBC's fantasy games which suggests that any Major League baseball player is associated" with the games, "or that any player endorses or sponsors the games in any way." She noted that "all fantasy game providers necessarily use names and playing records."[4]

The magistrate went on to say that even if Advanced Media (which represents almost all Major League players) had a right of publicity in their names and statistics, fantasy games are protected by the First Amendment, which outweighs the state-law right of publicity. She relied on a couple of precedents: a California case involving information and video clips that conveyed "bits of baseball history" (ironically, the information was provided by Major League Baseball Properties, Inc., and four individual players were the unsuccessful plaintiffs); and an Oklahoma case involving "CardToons," parody baseball cards that were protected by the First Amendment and thus could not be restrained even if they violated the right of publicity.[5]

Some might find it surprising that a fantasy game company found it necessary to go to court to establish its right to use publicly reported statistics. But the world of intellectual property is not always logical. What may seem obvious and commonsensical may not necessarily be the law; and even if the law favors the free speech side of the debate, industry practice, including the *in terrorem* effect of "cease and desist" letters, often squelches expression.[6] Kembrew McLeod, in his book *Freedom of Expression®*, and David Bollier in *Brand Name Bullies*, give hundreds of examples of questionable assertions of corporate control over common words, names, and images.[7]

## Can I Google This?

An equally dubious example of industry overreaching is Google's attempt to suppress the new verb "to google." As reported in an August 14, 2006 article in the British newspaper *The Independent*: "Search engine giant Google, known for its mantra 'don't be evil,' has fired off a series of legal letters to media organisations, warning them against using its name as a verb."[8]

According to *The Independent* and to a number of blog sites that picked up the story, Google wants to stop its name from entering the language as a verb because once the name becomes "generic," it can no longer be protected by trademark law. Hence, the term "genericide" for what would seem on the surface to be a stroke of luck: a brand becomes so popular that its name substitutes for the product or process itself. Historic examples include "Xerox," "Kleenex," and "band-aid."

Actually, Google has been sending cease and desist letters since 2003, when it tried to stop the lexicography site Wordspy from defining "google" as a verb synonymous with "search."[9] Accompanying that letter was a circular giving examples of proper and improper uses of the term, according to Google. This circular, which became the subject of understandable mockery in the blogosphere, attempts the impossible job of dictating how language should evolve. To wit:

*Appropriate:* "He ego-surfs on the Google search engine to see if he's listed in the results."

*Inappropriate:* "He googles himself."

and

*Appropriate:* "I ran a Google search to check out that guy from the party."

*Inappropriate:* "I googled that hottie."[10]

Shortly after the Wordspy episode, Google tried to persuade the publishers of the Oxford English Dictionary not to list its trademark as a word, but the effort was ultimately unavailing. According to Wikipedia, "The verb 'Google' was officially added to the Oxford English Dictionary on June 15, 2006, and to the eleventh edition of the Merriam-Webster Collegiate Dictionary in July, 2006."[11]

It's unlikely that Google would have a viable claim of trademark infringement or trademark dilution for ordinary written use of "google" as a verb. Trademark infringement requires commercial use and a likelihood of confusion; trademark dilution also doesn't apply to noncommercial uses, and courts have recognized First Amendment defenses. So, are Google's lawyers justified in sending out cease and desist letters that have scant legal basis?

Google's fear of "genericide" may provide some justification for the letters, even though it makes Google look both silly and untrue to its free-expression credo. In the long run, though, its attempt to stop the growth of language may be self-defeating as well as unsuccessful. As one blogger observed:

> How likely is Google to lose market share if they succeed in persuading people not to use their name as a verb? Very likely, actually. As long as people talk about googling for information, they will think of using Google first before other search engines. It's no mistake that as Google has increased its market share, the use of their name as a verb has increased throughout media and colloquial use.
>
> Is the potential loss of market share worth what Google will invest over the next 5-10 years to persuade people not to use their name as a verb? One has to wonder.[12]

August 16, 2006

**Update:** In October 2007, the U.S. Court of Appeals for the Eighth Circuit agreed that C.B.C. has a First Amendment right to distribute its fantasy games, writing: "the information used in CBC's fantasy baseball games is all readily available in the public domain, and it would be strange law that a person would not have a first amendment right to use information that is available to everyone."[13] In June 2008, the Supreme Court denied review, thus ending the case in fantasy baseball's favor.

## Notes

1. *C.B.C. Distribution Marketing v. Major League Baseball Advanced Media*, 443 F. Supp.2d 1077, 1091 (E.D. Mo. 2006).

2. *Carson v. Here's Johnny Portable Toilets, Inc.*, 698 F.2d 831 (6th Cir. 1983).

3. *Zacchini v. Scripps-Howard Broadcasting Co.*, 433 U.S. 562 (1977).

4. *C.B.C. Distribution and Marketing, supra*, 443 F. Supp.2d at 1086.

5. *Gionfriddo v. Major League Baseball*, 94 Cal. App.4th 400 (2001); *CardToons v. Major League Baseball Players Association*, 95 F.3d 959 (10th Cir. 1996).

6. See Marjorie Heins & Tricia Beckles, *Will Fair Use Survive? Free Expression in the Age of Copyright Control* (Free Expression Policy Project/Brennan Center for Justice, 2006), 4, http://ncac.org/fepp-articles/will-fair-use-survive-free-expression-in-the-age-of-copyright-control.

7. Kembrew McLeod, *Freedom of Expression®: Resistance and Repression in the Age of Intellectual Property* (2007); David Bollier, *Brand Name Bullies: The Quest to Own and Control Culture* (2006).

8. Stephen Foley, "To google or not to google? It's a legal question," *The Independent*, 8/14/2006.

9. Email from Wordspy manager Paul McFedries to the American Dialect Society mailing list, quoting the text of Google's letter, http://listserv.linguistlist.org/cgi-bin/wa?A2=ind0302D&L=ads-l&P=R2450 (accessed 2006).

10. See Frank Ahrens, "So Google Is No Brand X, but What Is 'Genericide'?," *Washington Post*, 8/5/2006, D01, http://www.washingtonpost.com/wp-dyn/content/article/2006/08/04/AR2006080401536.html; "This word just in…," posted by Doug, 7/10/2006, http://xooglers.blogspot.com/2006/07/this-word-just-in.html (accessed 2006) (both quoting the Google memo).

11. http://en.wikipedia.org/wiki/Google.

12. "Google emulates Xerox debacle: asks *Washington Post* not to…," posted by Michael Martinez, 8/9/06, http://www.seomoz.org/blogdetail.php?ID=1274 (accessed 2006).

13. *C.B.C. Distribution Marketing v. Major League Baseball Advanced Media*, 505 F.3d 818, 823 (8th Cir. 2007).

# Blanche DuBois Meets the Copyright Cops

Blanche DuBois, the fragile, self-deluding southern belle in Tennessee Williams's 1947 play, *A Streetcar Named Desire*, is one of the great tragic characters in American literature. But who owns Blanche, and can the holder of the copyright in *Streetcar* stop a creative artist from impersonating her, as the author, actor and sometime gay/female impersonator Mark Sam Rosenthal does in his recent performance piece, *Blanche Survives Katrina in a FEMA Trailer Named Desire*?

The University of the South in Sewanee, Tennessee, the holder of the *Streetcar* copyright, thinks it can. On September 3, 2008, lawyers for the University sent Rosenthal a cease and desist letter asserting complete ownership of *Streetcar*, "including, without limitation, the dialogue, plot, and characters Blanche DuBois, Stanley Kowalski, and Stella Kowalski." The letter demanded that Rosenthal "cease and desist from any and all use and exploitation of the performance piece, including without limitation stage production, website and any other promotion," unless he gets a license from the University.

*Blanche Survives Katrina*, which was a hit at the recent International Fringe Theater Festival in New York City, imagines Blanche anachronistically trapped in her illusions, pretensions, and exaggerated femininity as she confronts the devastation of Hurricane Katrina and its aftermath: homelessness, fast food, minimum-wage work, and evangelistic megachurches. Reviewers called the piece "funny and poignant"; "a humorous yet bitterly sad meditation on the desperate conditions during a national disaster where government relief was inept at best, criminal at worst"; and "a thoughtful, laugh-out-loud story based on one film icon's descent into reality."[1] (The 1951 film version of *Streetcar* starred Vivien Leigh at her fragile, deluded best, and newcomer Marlon Brando, who also starred in the original stage production, as an unforgettably *macho* Stanley Kowalski, Blanche's nemesis.)

Rosenthal is hardly the first artist to have appropriated a character from *A Streetcar Named Desire* in order to make his or her own commentary on American politics and culture. In 1990, the lesbian performance team Split Britches created an equally gender-bending look at *Streetcar*, called *Belle Reprieve*. The Split Britches Web site describes *Belle Reprieve* as a "steamy and hysterical" examination of "the mythic proportions of Stanley and Blanche," which "both honors Williams and turns him on his head."[2] Whether the creators of such fictional commentaries must seek permission from and pay fees to the holder of the copyright in *Streetcar* is primarily a question of "fair use" under copyright law.

Fair use allows artists to borrow characters, plot elements, and even text, without seeking permission, when their purpose is commentary, critique, or other "transformative" use. The principle of fair use is particularly important for critiques and parodies that would not likely get the approval (and therefore permission) of the copyright owner. The Supreme Court has called fair use one of the most important safety valves for free expression in a copyright system that otherwise gives monopoly control over creative works to their owners, although for limited periods of time.[3]

The Supreme Court described the concept of transformative use in a 1994 case involving a parody rap music version of the Roy Orbison song "Oh Pretty Woman." When an artist uses elements of a copyrighted work for purposes such as criticism, commentary, or news reporting, the Court said, the question is whether the new work

> "merely supersede[s] the objects" of the original creation, or instead adds something new, with a further purpose or different character, altering the first with new expression, meaning, or message; it asks, in other words, whether and to what extent the new work is "transformative." Although such transformative use is not absolutely necessary for a finding of fair use, the goal of copyright, to promote science and the arts, is generally furthered by the creation of transformative works. Such works thus lie at the heart of the fair use doctrine's guarantee of breathing space within the confines of copyright, and the more transformative the new work, the less will be the significance of other factors, like commercialism, that may weigh against a finding of fair use.[4]

In this case, the Court strongly suggested that the rap music version of "Oh Pretty Woman" was a transformative, African American-inflected parody of Orbison's "white bread" original, and thus, was fair use within the meaning of the law.

The case that is probably closest to the facts of *Blanche Survives Katrina* involved a battle between the owners of the rights to Margaret Mitchell's classic Civil War novel, *Gone With the Wind*, and the publishers of a contemporary novel called *The Wind Done Gone*, which took most of the characters and plot elements of Mitchell's story and essentially turned them upside down, exposing the racism of the original. Although the Mitchell estate initially won an injunction against publication of *The Wind Done Gone,* that injunction was vacated on appeal; the appeals court said an injunction was not warranted, because the case for fair use was very strong.

Emphasizing the importance of fair use as a free-expression safeguard, the appeals court in *The Wind Done Gone* case said that fair use is important because it allows "later authors to use a previous author's copyright to introduce new ideas or concepts to the public." The court found the parody element in *The Wind Done Gone* to be clear: the novel "is not a general commentary upon the Civil-War-era American South, but a specific criticism of and rejoinder to the depiction of slavery and the relationships between blacks and whites in *Gone With the Wind*." The later novel, the court said, attempts "to explode the romantic, idealized portrait of the antebellum South during and after the Civil War."[5]

Whether or not *Blanche Survives Katrina* qualifies as a parody or critique of *A Streetcar Named Desire* in the same way that *The Wind Done Gone* qualified as a parody/critique of *Gone With the Wind*, Rosenthal's performance piece is certainly transformative. It also uses much less of the original work than *The Wind Done Gone* used in its send-up of Margaret Mitchell's classic (which was, incidentally, also made into a movie starring Vivien Leigh). In fact, it is possible that a court would find that *Blanche Survives Katrina* does not even use enough of *Streetcar* to meet the test of "substantial similarity" under copyright law. Without "substantial similarity," there is no copyright violation.

Cease and desist letters can be intimidating to artists, who are not experts in copyright law and who often lack the financial means to hire attorneys to advise and defend them. Rosenthal has sought and obtained *pro bono* legal help, however, and his lawyers (at the firm of Orrick, Herrington & Sutcliffe) have responded to the cease and desist letter by asking the University's lawyers to specify the nature of their claims, including an explanation of why the fair use doctrine would not apply.

For Rosenthal, who left a career in corporate advertising when, as his Web site explains, "his sick sense of humor cried out for spiritual release," resisting the copyright owner's demands is important. He first performed *Blanche Survives Katrina* at the 2007 HOT! Festival of Queer Culture. Blanche, often called "America's most broken woman," is "the role of his dreams."[6]

September 22, 2008

**Update:** In January 2009, *Blanche Survives Katrina* began a commercial run at the SoHo Playhouse in New York. Lawyers for the University of the South continued to press their copyright claims by sending another cease and desist letter on January 22.[7]

## Notes

1.  Caraid O'Brien, "The Kindness of FEMA," 8/15/2008, http://www.offoffoff.com/theater/2008/blanche_ survives_katrina_in_a_fema_trailer_named_desire. php; "Blanche Survives Katrina Opens at SoHo Playhouse," *Broadway World*, 1/25/2009, https:// www.broadwayworld.com/off-broadway/article/ BLANCHE-SURVIVES-KATRINA-Opens-At-SoHo-Playhouse-125-20090125. See also Anita Gates, "No Kindness for Strangers at the Superdome,"

*NY Times*, 1/29/2009, who was less enthusiastic, http://www.nytimes.com/2009/01/29/theater/reviews/29blan.html.

2. See http://www.split-britches.com/archive for more about *Belle Reprieve* and other productions by Split Britches.

3. The time limits have become more theoretical than actual: see "The Frozen Public Domain," in this volume; and Marjorie Heins & Tricia Beckles, *Will Fair Use Survive? Free Expression in the Age of Copyright Control* (Free Expression Policy Project/Brennan Center for Justice, 2005), http://ncac.org/fepp-articles/will-fair-use-survive-free-expression-in-the-age-of-copyright-control-full-report.

4. *Campbell v. Acuff-Rose*, 510 U.S. 569, 579 (1994) (citations omitted).

5. *Suntrust v. Houghton Mifflin Co.*, 268 F.3d 1257, 1264-69 (11th Cir. 2001).

6. Rosenthal's Web site: http://blanchesurviveskatrina.com (accessed 2008).

7. Patrick Healy, "One Man's Blanche is a University's Infringement," *NY Times*, 2/4/2009, http://www.nytimes.com/2009/02/05/theater/05ceas.html.

# Trashing the Copyright Balance (Music Sampling)

Copyright law is a tricky balancing act. So it's understandable that a federal appeals court recently threw up its hands, refused to balance the rights of copyright owners against those of innovative rap musicians and their audiences, and flatly announced that sampling even one note from a previous musical recording would automatically be a copyright infringement.

The case involved a two-second guitar chord from the rap song "Get Off Your Ass and Jam," by Funkadelic, modified to lower the pitch, then "looped" to appear five times in the song "100 Miles and Runnin'" by N.W.A. A typical enough incidence of sampling, which is after all a basic component of hip hop music.[1] (For that matter, the borrowing of themes, chords, and melodies has always been a common occurrence in all musical genres.)

In a lawsuit brought by Bridgeport Music, Inc. and other owners of "Get Off Your Ass," a federal judge found that N.W.A.'s borrowing of one chord to be *"de minimis"* and therefore not a violation of copyright law. But two weeks ago, the U.S. Court of Appeals for the Sixth Circuit reversed that decision. It did so by interpreting the section of the copyright law that applies to sound recordings to impose liability even if only one note of a previous recording is borrowed.[2] That makes things simple for the music industry, but it also chills a lot of artistic expression, especially in the envelope-pushing genre of rap, and it's profoundly wrong as a matter of copyright principles.

Borrowing and copying didn't originate with rap or any other musical genre; they are time-honored practices in all the creative arts. Justice Joseph Story wrote over a century ago: "Every book in literature, science and art, borrows, and must necessarily borrow, and use much which was well known and used before."[3] From classical music to jazz and rock and roll, Impressionism to Surrealist collage and Pop Art, appropriation is a standard building block of creativity.

Copyright law acknowledges the importance of creative copying in two primary ways: the fair use doctrine, and the concept of *de minimis* borrowing. Although fair use was recognized early on as an important factor in determining the legality of sampling, courts have more frequently looked to the *de minimis* defense. Where so little is taken that the new work wouldn't reasonably be thought to undermine the value of the original, then the borrowing is *de minimis*, and not a violation of copyright.

The *de minimis* rule serves the purpose of copyright law in balancing the rights of owners and borrowers. As the lower court explained in the *Bridgeport Music* case:

> The Court recognizes that the fact of blatant copying is not challenged by the defendant ..., and that the purpose of the copyright laws is to deter wholesale plagiarism of prior works. However, a balance must be struck between protecting an artist's interests, and depriving other artists of the building blocks of future works. Since the advent of Western music, musicians have freely borrowed themes and ideas from other musicians.[4]

The court of appeals' decision to reject this balancing approach is understandable. Balancing is difficult, and in copyright law, there are few "bright lines," so one never knows for sure whether one's copying will in fact turn out to be *de minimis*, fair use, or otherwise legitimate. Anyway, the industry already has a system in place that takes care of the logistics of getting permissions for musical samples, so why not require everyone to use it?

The problem with this is that it ignores the critical pivot on which copyright law is built: the balance between monopoly control and free expression. Not all good music today is created in entertainment industry studios. Independent artists, artists who can't afford fees, and rebels who just don't want to get permission for every chord or riff they copy, are silenced in a system that ignores their free speech rights.

In addition, requiring permission—in the absence of a legal mandate of compulsory licensing— means that copyright owners can censor, denying permission to anyone whose musical message they dislike. This was exactly the situation fifteen years ago when the owners of Roy Orbison's classic "Oh Pretty Woman" denied permission to a raunchy rap group named Two Live Crew to record their irreverent version of the song. The Supreme Court ruled that Two Live Crew probably didn't need permission, because their vulgar version was a parody—a "transformative" use—of the "white bread" original.[5]

Parody is one common form of fair use under copyright law—others being scholarship, criticism, news reporting, and even wholesale copying of TV programs onto videotape for viewing at a later time. Oddly, the Sixth Circuit in the *Bridgeport* case did not even mention fair use. The judges may have mistakenly thought that without the element of parody, as in the Two Live Crew case, there is no fair use defense to copyright infringement, even when the use that's made of the copyright-protected music is transformative, as it almost always is with hip hop, because the samples are, by definition, woven into a new work.

Essentially, fair use is simply a question (in the words of one venerable judge) of whether copying "has been done to an unfair extent."[6] Some of the factors that go into the analysis are: how much material is copied; whether it is the most important or essential part of the original work; whether the use is transformative; and the effect on the market for the original work—but this decidedly does not include the possible dampening of demand because of a critical review or a wicked parody.

Fair use is especially important in enriching our culture because it encourages new works. As the Supreme Court has said: "The immediate effect of our copyright law is to secure a fair return for an 'author's' creative labor. But the ultimate aim, by this incentive, is to stimulate artistic creativity for the general public good."[7] The *Bridgeport* decision sadly ignores this basic principle in its effort to stamp out sampling that's not approved by copyright owners. Hopefully, the losing lawyers will ask for rehearing, or for Supreme Court review.

September 21, 2004

**Update:** On December 20, 2004, the Sixth Circuit Court of Appeals granted a petition for rehearing in this case. At the same time, the court amended its opinion to indicate that it did not mean to eliminate the fair use defense in sound recording cases—only to eliminate the *de minimis* rule. The Recording Industry Association of America had filed a brief in support of rehearing, arguing that the court's interpretation of the law was "novel and unsustainable."[8]

On June 3, 2005, the same three judges who wrote the

first decision issued their new decision on rehearing. It was essentially the same as the original decision and ignored the arguments of both the defendant, No Limit Films, and of the Brennan Center for Justice and the Electronic Frontier Foundation, which filed a friend of the court brief.[9]

## Notes

1. Hip hop and rap are not exactly the same thing, although in this article I use the terms interchangeably. According to one aficionado, hip hop is "a music genre consisting of a stylized rhythmic music that commonly accompanies rapping, a rhythmic and rhyming speech that is chanted." Music Fans Beta, https://musicfans.stackexchange. com/questions/65/what-is-the-difference-between-hip-hop-and-rap. Another definition on the same Web site explains: "Rapping is often associated with and a primary ingredient of hip hop music, but the origins of the phenomenon can be said to predate hip hop culture by centuries. So Rap would be a Speech and Hip Hop a Genre. Also, Rap is more about the poetry of words and word styles and Hip Hop is more about the music (beats)."

2. *Bridgeport Music, Inc. v. Dimension Films*, 383 F.3d 390 (6th Cir. 2004), as amended after rehearing, 410 F.3d 792 (2005).

3. *Emerson v. Davies*, 8 F. Cas. 615, 619 (No. 4,436) (C.C.D. Mass. 1845).

4. *Bridgeport Music, Inc. v. Dimension Films*, 230 F. Supp.2d 830, 842 (M.D. Tenn. 2002), reversed, 410 F.3d 792 (6th Cir. 2005).

5.  *Campbell v. Acuff-Rose Music, Inc.*, 510 U.S. 569 (1994).

6.  Judge Learned Hand in *West Publishing Co. v. Edward Thompson Co.*, 169 F. 833, 861 (E.D.N.Y. 1909).

7.  *Twentieth Century Music Corp. v. Aiken*, 422 U.S. 151, 156 (1975).

8.  *Amicus* Recording Industry Association of America's Brief in Support of Petition for Rehearing, *Bridgeport Music v. No Limit Films*, No. 02-6521 (Sept. 21, 2004), 1.

9.  *Bridgeport Music, Inc. v. Dimension Films*, 410 F.3d 792 (6th Cir. 2005).

# The Frozen Public Domain

On January 15, 2003, the Supreme Court decided *Eldred v. Ashcroft*. By a vote of 7-2, the Court upheld the 1998 "Sonny Bono Copyright Term Extension Act," a law that lengthened the term of copyright protection across the board for twenty years—for a total of ninety-five years for corporations, and life plus seventy years for individuals and their heirs. The law means that creative works dating back to the 1920s and '30s—songs by Cole Porter, books by F. Scott Fitzgerald, and, probably of most concern to the entertainment industry, cartoon characters by Walt Disney—will not enter the public domain for another twenty years.

Justice Ruth Bader Ginsburg wrote a dry, legalistic opinion for the seven justices who joined in the majority opinion. She made no mention of the myriad ways that a stagnant public domain impoverishes art and culture, even though dozens of organizations such as the College Art Association had submitted friend of the court (or *amicus curiae*) briefs describing how important it is for older works to enter the public domain. Once freed of copyright controls, these old movies, songs, books, and historical documents become available to everyone from archivists to jazz fans, to access, reproduce, distribute, and enjoy.

Instead, Ginsburg's majority opinion harshly critiqued Justice Stephen Breyer, one of the two dissenters, for making "policy arguments" instead of sticking to legal precedent. Breyer's impassioned dissent did indeed rely on those *amicus curiae* briefs, which documented the dangers of locking up culture under the monopoly control of media corporations, or else (for works that are no longer commercially profitable) in a legal limbo where permission to reproduce copyrighted works is hard to come by because their owners cannot even be found. Breyer noted, for example, that about 350,000 films, songs, and other works with little or no commercial value are still frozen in "a kind of intellectual purgatory" because of the Sonny Bono law.[1]

According to Justice Ginsburg's opinion, Congress has near-total discretion to decide what is an appropriate copyright term. The decision leaves Congress free to extend yet again the "limited time" that the Constitution's Copyright Clause specifies should be allowed for monopoly control of creative works. As Justice John Paul Stevens, the Court's other dissenter, pointed out, only one year's worth of books, musical compositions, movies, or other works of visual art have entered the public domain in the past eighty years. By allowing Congress to extend existing copyrights *ad infinitum*, Stevens said, Justice Ginsburg's majority opinion ignored "the central purpose" of the Copyright Clause.[2]

Ginsburg was certainly right that copyright term extension is a matter for Congress to decide, but that doesn't disqualify the courts, in adjudicating the constitutionality of laws, from weighing in with policy considerations. The U.S. Constitution is filled with Delphic phrases that must be interpreted in light of current political realities. Under the reign of Chief Justice William Rehnquist in particular, the Supreme Court has engaged in elaborate policy debates and invalidated laws that it has found inconsistent with its views on public policy. Likewise in the "Sonny Bono" case, the term "limited times" calls out for some judicial interpretation of what can reasonably be considered "limited," in light of the overarching goals of Copyright Clause. As Justice Breyer pointed out, judicial oversight is necessary in order to "avoid the monopolies and consequent restrictions of expression" that the Copyright Clause and the First Amendment were both intended to guard against.[3]

Despite the disappointingly wooden Supreme Court decision in *Eldred*, the case has actually had a salutary effect. It took the disappearing public domain out of the legislative shadows and into the bright light of policy debate. A remarkable coalition of scholars, libraries, writers, archivists, and cyber-activists joined in fighting the Sonny Bono law. This coalition just might be able to persuade Congress to revisit the issue of our frozen public domain. Legislation allowing copyrights that have no commercial value to lapse, for example, would free up many thousands of historical documents and other works.

Meanwhile, artists, critics, Web entrepreneurs, and others are likely to make even greater use of free expression "safety valves" within the copyright system, such as the doctrine of fair use. Fair use allows the reproduction of copyrighted works for purposes of scholarship, comment, news reports, and parody. Heaven knows, there is much to parody in our present culture, including the Supreme Court's tone-deaf decision in the *Eldred* case.

January 17, 2003

## Notes

1. *Eldred v. Ashcroft*, 537 U.S. 186, 199 (2003) (majority opinion); 242-67 (Breyer dissent).

2. *Id.*, 222-42 (Stevens dissent).

3. *Id.*, 264 (Breyer dissent).

# The Joyce Saga - Literary Heirs & Copyright Abuse

An article in this week's *New Yorker* magazine chronicles the aggressive activities of James Joyce's grandson Stephen in suppressing Joyce scholarship, not only by refusing permission to quote copyrighted writings, but by asserting control over materials that aren't even part of the James Joyce estate. Such materials include letters from friends of Joyce, medical records of Joyce's daughter Lucia, and the 1922 first edition of Joyce's great novel *Ulysses*, which is now in the public domain.[1]

Coinciding with a lawsuit filed by the Stanford Center for Internet and Society against the Joyce estate, the article publicizes a problem that has long been known in the literary world: the tendency of some heirs to use copyright as a lever to control what is said, or not said, about their famous ancestors.

The plaintiff in the suit is literary scholar Carol Shloss, whose 2003 book, *Lucia Joyce: To Dance in the Wake*, was drastically cut by her publisher, Farrar, Straus and Giroux, in response to threats from Stephen Joyce. More than thirty pages of quotations were excised, according to the complaint filed in federal court in San Francisco, which asserts that as a consequence, the book lacked strong documentation, and reviews faulted it as being more "wish fulfillment" than scholarship.[2]

Shloss now wants to amplify the record by posting a Web site with the excised quotes, keyed to passages in the text of her book where they should have appeared. Stephen and the estate wrote to Shloss, to Stanford University where she teaches, and to the Center for Internet and Society forbidding use of the material—some of which, according to the federal court complaint, is not even within the estate's copyright, and the rest of which, they say, is fair use.

What gives particular flavor to this case is Stephen Joyce's uniquely nasty and bullying style, combined with the iconic status of his grandfather in the literary canon. *Ulysses* may be difficult reading (and *Finnegan's Wake* verges on the incomprehensible), but both are inspired, lyrical, and heroic in their ambitions. Joyce encouraged commentary; in addition, he was a free speech champion because he opened up literary expression to the full range of human experience, both spiritual and carnal, and as a consequence was the target of obscenity prosecutions. *Ulysses* was banned in both England and America until the 1930s. So it is ironic that Joyce's grandson has made a career out of attempting to stifle, control, and leverage his copyright power to exact various concessions from librarians and scholars as a condition of quoting any of his grandfather's words.

In addition to seeking a judgment that will allow Shloss's Web site to go public, the lawsuit alleges that the conduct of Stephen and the estate amounts to copyright abuse. A finding of abuse would be a big step toward encouraging copyright bullies to be more circumspect in their efforts to censor scholarship in the future.

June 15, 2006

**Update:** In February 2007, the federal district court denied the defendants' motion to dismiss the case. In addition to finding that there was a live controversy, the court ruled that Shloss stated a viable claim against Stephen Joyce for

207

"copyright misuse." The following month, Stephen and the Joyce Estate settled the case by agreeing not to sue Shloss for publishing any of the materials in question. The only limitation is that any Web publication "must be accessible only within the United States to computer with a U.S. Internet Protocol ("IP") address."[3]

In May 2009, the federal court ordered the Joyce estate to pay Shloss more than $326,000 in attorney's fees. The Stanford Fair Use Project reported the following September that "after initially appealing that decision to the Ninth Circuit, the Estate thought better of it and agreed to pay $240,000 in fees to resolve the matter once and for all."[4]

## Notes

1. D.T. Max, "The Injustice Collector, *New Yorker*, 6/19/2006, https://www.newyorker.com/magazine/2006/06/19/the-injustice-collector; see also Order Denying Defendants' Motion to Dismiss (N.D. Cal. 2007), restating the plaintiff's allegations, http://cyberlaw.stanford.edu/files/blogs/Order%20denying%20Motion%20to%20Dismiss.pdf.

2. Complaint for Declaratory Judgment and Injunctive Relief, *Shloss v. Joyce* (N.D. Cal. 1/25/2007), https://www.scribd.com/document/2615300/Shloss-v-Joyce-Document-No-1; see also Shloss v. Estate of Joyce, http://cyberlaw.stanford.edu/our-work/cases/shloss-v-estate-joyce.

3. *Schloss* Settlement Agreement, http://cyberlaw.stanford. edu/files/blogs/Shloss%20Settlement%20Agreement. pdf; "Stanford Scholar Wins Right to Publish Joyce Material in Copyright Suit Led by Stanford Law School's Fair Use Project" (press release), 3/22/2007, http://cyberlaw.stanford.edu/files/blogs/Shloss%20 Press%20Release.pdf.

4. *Shloss v. Estate of Joyce* (Center for Internet and Society), http://cyberlaw.stanford.edu/our-work/cases/shloss-v-estate-joyce.

# Acknowledgments

I was lucky to have friends and colleagues in the community of free speech advocates who supported my vision for a little think tank that would delve into the social policy issues that drive the seemingly eternal human impulse to censor. First and foremost was Joan Bertin, who was an inexhaustible source of wise advice when we were both attorneys at the ACLU, and who then, as director of the National Coalition Against Censorship (NCAC), was my partner in creating FEPP and raising the funds to get it started.

Stephanie Elizondo Griest, founder of the Youth Free Expression Program, was my assistant at NCAC; she was dedicated, brilliant, conscientious, and funny. Svetlana Mintcheva, who became NCAC's first arts advocate, was a colleague and friend over many years of working our way through convoluted free speech controversies. Christina Cho contributed her superlative research and writing skills to FEPP's early policy reports, *Media Literacy: An Alternative to Censorship* and *Free Expression in Arts Funding*. Kim Commerato and Elizabeth Weill-Greenberg provided further valuable research on the arts funding report. FEPP's first research fellow, Nancy Kranich, researched and wrote a comprehensive report on the theory and reality of the rapidly growing alternatives to a profit-oriented, closed, and costly system of expression: *The Information Commons: A Public Policy Report*.

Foundation officers with real vision and a long view about the challenges posed by free speech advocacy helped FEPP get started, and kept it going for its first seven years. These prescient supporters, who were also wise counselors, included Margaret Ayers of the Robert Sterling Clark Foundation, Arch Gillies, Joel Wachs, and Pamela Clapp of the Andy Warhol Foundation for the Visual Arts, Joan Shigekawa of the Rockefeller Foundation, Claudine Brown of the Nathan Cummings Foundation, and Gara LaMarche of the Open Society Institute.

Tom Gerety, then director of the Brennan Center for Justice, was responsible for adding FEPP to the Center's Democracy Program in 2004. Deborah Goldberg, then head of the Democracy Program, was a welcoming boss. Brennan Center research associates Tricia Beckles and Neema Trivedi provided expert assistance and eagerly plunged into some daunting research projects.

Also at the Brennan Center, research fellow and IP expert Laura Quilter conducted an extensive survey of how universities and other Internet service providers were responding to cease and desist letters and copyright take-down notices; Laura put it all together in the report *Intellectual Property and Free Speech in the Online World*. Brennan Center attorney Ciara Torres-Spelliscy authored our submission to the Lincoln, Nebraska Broadband Task Force on the importance of allowing public utilities, not just private entrepreneurs, to provide Internet access to their communities. The Media Access Project, Common Cause, and other groups joined in the submission.

Colleagues who generously assisted FEPP with expertise, advice, and ideas included Frank Baker, Rob Balin, Kelly Barsdate, Cary Bazalgette, Roberto Bedoya, Barton Beebe, Thomas Birch, Wally Bowen, James Boyle, Ann Brick, Bethany Bryson, David Buckingham, Diane Cabell, Adan Canizales, Bob Clarida, Michelle Coe, Cindy Cohn,

David Considine, Mark Cooper, Frank Couvares, Paul DiMaggio, Jennifer Dowley, Barry Duncan, Maryo Ewell, Gary Ferrington, Seth Finkelstein, Jib Fowles, Eric Freedman, Jonathan Freedman, Todd Gitlin, Michael Godwin, Jeffrey Goldstein, Wendy Gordon, Jennifer Granick, David Greene, Chris Hansen, Bennett Haselton, Jesse Hofrichter, Robert Horwitz, Sam Howard-Spink, Justin Hughes, Aziz Huq, Peter Jaszi, Joan Jeffri, Henry Jenkins, Burt Joseph, Judith Krug, Lawrence Lessig, Nan Levinson, Robert Lynch, Mike Males, Bob McCannon, Claire Montgomery, Norma Munn, Brian Newman, David Nimmer, Julian Petley, Richard Rhodes, Marieli Rowe, Virginia Rutledge, Andy Schwartzman, Wendy Seltzer, Carroll Seron, Steve Shapiro, Larry Siems, Eve Sinaiko, David Sobel, Steven Tepper, Elizabeth Thoman, Peter Tsapatsaris, Siva Vaidhyanathan, Julie Van Camp, Fred von Lohmann, Patricia Wright, Diane Zimmerman, and my beloved mentor, now sadly deceased, Judge Benjamin Kaplan.

Finally, a big thanks to Aaron Lisman, who designed the FEPP Web site, taught me enough hypertext markup language so that I could (for the most part) manage the site, and, long after he'd moved on to other professional commitments, generously spared time to rescue me from electronic disaster when I screwed something up.

# Index

Beethoven, Ludwig van, 132; Emperor Concerto, 134
Benhabib, Seyla, 165
Bernstein, Leonard (*West Side Story*), 134
Bertelsmann, 149
Bertin, Joan, 2-3, 210
*Bethel School District v. Fraser,* 70-71, 74n
Billboard Music Awards, 89
Birth control, 119, 156
*Bishop v. Aronov,* 52n
Blackmail, 3, 64, 130
Blackmun, Harry (Justice), 125-26n
Blasphemy, 33-34, 117
*Bloomberg News,* 166-67
*The Blues* (film): see Scorsese, Martin
*Board of Education, Island Trees School District v. Pico,* 20n, 122-24, 125n
Boccaccio (*Decameron*), 119
Bollier, David (*Brand Name Bullies*), 186
Bollinger, Lee, 167
Bono, 81, 87-88, 150
Bowdler, Henrietta, 127-31
Bowdler, Thomas, 127-31
Bradbury, Ray (*Fahrenheit 451*), 150
Brandeis, Louis (Justice), 37
*Brandenburg v. Ohio,* 37n
Brando, Marlon, 192
Brecht, Bertolt (*The Rise and Fall of the City of Mahagonny*), 132, 134
Brennan, William (Justice), 27, 125-26n
Brennan Center for Justice at NYU School of Law, 3, 8, 201, 211
Breyer, Stephen (Justice), 45-47,

73, 98, 203-05
Bridgeport Music, Inc., 197-201
*Bridgeport Music, Inc. v. Dimension Films,* 198-99, 201nn, 202n
Broadcasting: see media democracy; structural free expression issues; United States, Federal Communications Commission
Brooklyn Museum, 18
Brown, Claudine, 211
*Brown v. Entertainment Merchants Ass'n,* 100n
Bruckner, Anton, 132
*Burstyn v. Wilson,* 15, 19n, 20nn, 37n
Bush, George W. (President), 149, 154, 157; administration of, 82, 84, 152-60
Bush, Jeb (Governor), 142, 148-49, 150
*Butler v. Michigan,* 19n

Cage, John, 109
Cage, Xenia, 109
California: intellectual property case, 186; loyalty oath, 28-29; legislature, 53-54; video game law, 93, 97-98
Campaign finance regulation, 4
Cancer, 156, 158
*CardToons v. Major League Baseball Players Association,* 189n
Carlin, George ("Filthy Words" monolog), 77-78, 104-05
*Campbell v. Acuff-Rose,* 196n, 202n
*Carmen,* 13
Carrington, Leonora, 108
Carson, Johnny, 185
*Carson v. Here's Johnny Portable Toilets,* 189n
Carter Center, 46

216